PREFACE

1973-83

During the past ten years, there has been growing interest in regional cooperation schemes in the Pacific Basin area. Five OECD Member countries (Australia, Canada, Japan, New Zealand and the United States) are located in the zone; some of the world's fastest growing newly-industrialised nations border the Pacific; more than a dozen developing countries are also Pacific nations. The issues that are at the centre of policy research in relation to Pacific Basin cooperation are indeed the crucial questions of development: investment strategies, energy resource management, raw materials, human resources, food security and transport infrastructure. It is all the more crucial for the developing countries of the zone who find themselves in a complex and unique configuration of complementarity and competition with the industrial and newly-industrialised nations of the region.

The Development Centre undertook this study of Pacific Basin regional economic integration to provide an account of the concept as it has developed over the past twenty years. The arguments advanced are detailed and cited in their historical context; economic sectoral arguments are reviewed and presented. An effort is made to up-date existing literature in the field in order to show the evolution of the concept in academic and policy circles of the region.

The purpose of the study has been to make available to a wide public the arguments that have been put forward for economic integration in the Pacific region, especially to readers outside of the area who are unfamiliar with recent developments there.

If indeed the Asia-Pacific zone is to be a major theatre of economic development in the coming years, as appears increasingly evident, it is imperative that more insight be gained and knowledge disseminated relating to the internal mechanics of regional interdependence.

During the early years of the Organisation for European Economic Cooperation, the predecessor of the present Organisation for Economic Cooperation and Development, many of the same hopes and fears were expressed concerning that new organisation as are now heard from Pacific Basin advocates and sceptics. It is therefore opportune that the Development Centre of the OECD draw attention to Pacific Basin cooperation efforts and continue to monitor their progress; much of what is now so passionately debated for that region has both historical roots and institutional precedent.

The Development Centre will seek to participate in the analysis, discussion and interpretation of the rapidly changing economic scene in the Pacific region and its impact on the world beyond.

Just FAALAND
President
OECD Development Centre
July 1983

LIST OF CONTENTS

DEVELOPMENT CENTRE STUDIES

DEVELOPMENT CENTRE
OF THE ORGANISATION FOR ECONOMIC CO-OPERATION AND DEVELOPMENT

Pursuant to article 1 of the Convention signed in Paris on 14th December, 1960, and which came into force on 30th September, 1961, the Organisation for Economic Co-operation and Development (OECD) shall promote policies designed:

- to achieve the highest sustainable economic growth and employment and a rising standard of living in Member countries, while maintaining financial stability, and thus to contribute to the development of the world economy;
- to contribute to sound economic expansion in Member as well as non-member countries in the process of economic development; and
- to contribute to the expansion of world trade on a multilateral, non-discriminatory basis in accordance with international obligations.

The Signatories of the Convention on the OECD are Austria, Belgium, Canada, Denmark, France, the Federal Republic of Germany, Greece, Iceland, Ireland, Italy, Luxembourg, the Netherlands, Norway, Portugal, Spain, Sweden, Switzerland, Turkey, the United Kingdom and the United States. The following countries acceded subsequently to this Convention (the dates are those on which the instruments of accession were deposited): Japan (28th April, 1964), Finland (28th January, 1969), Australia (7th June, 1971) and New Zealand (29th May, 1973).

The Socialist Federal Republic of Yugoslavia takes part in certain work of the OECD (agreement of 28th October, 1961).

The Development Centre of the Organisation for Economic Co-operation and Development was established by decision of the OECD Council on 23rd October, 1962.

The purpose of the Centre is to bring together the knowledge and experience available in Member countries of both economic development and the formulation and execution of general policies of economic aid; to adapt such knowledge and experience to the actual needs of countries or regions in the process of development and to put the results at the disposal of the countries by appropriate means.

The Centre has a special and autonomous position within the OECD which enables it to enjoy scientific independence in the execution of its task. Nevertheless, the Centre can draw upon the experience and knowledge available in the OECD in the development field.

Publié en français sous le titre :

**LA COOPÉRATION ÉCONOMIQUE
DANS LE BASSIN PACIFIQUE**

THE OPINIONS EXPRESSED AND ARGUMENTS EMPLOYED
IN THIS PUBLICATION ARE THE RESPONSIBILITY OF THE AUTHORS AND
DO NOT NECESSARILY REPRESENT THOSE OF THE OECD

INTRODUCTION

The idea of a broad coordinating body for Pacific trade and economic development first came from Japan, in the form of academic research and unofficial policy advice in the mid-1960s. What arose as a plan for 'free-trade zones' (Pacific Area Free Trade Association or PAFTA) in the region, soon took shape as an organisational concept which stressed the growing interdependences of the area and the mutual interests in larger cooperation on a regional basis in the Pacific. The key word in the debate was 'interdependence'.[1] This word reflects well the changing discourse at policy level during the late 1960s and early 1970s. The first decade of development emphasised the element of dependence in relationships, and the governing concept was 'aid'. This essentially didactic posture on the part of the industrial countries changed only with experience in the field. The constitution of a serious negotiating cartel in the form of OPEC in the 1970s brought further changes in attitude as the promising growth rates of the 1960s began to slow down. Also, progress towards economic union in Western Europe showed a way to concrete forms of economic cooperation, and brought nearer to maturity a new force in the economic and political world of the industrial nations, that of a United Europe. The spectacular rise of post-war Japan to industrial might completed the trilateral balance of economic power in the North. It also shifted economic power away from a purely Atlantic base.

---

1. For an overview of this approach, see the recent OECD publication World Economic Interdependence and the Evolving North-South Relationship, Paris, 1983.

I. THE CONCEPT OF PACIFIC BASIN COOPERATION

A. The Pacific Region

The Pacific region is not a homogeneous economic, social or political unit. Its development problems have been quite different from those of Africa or Latin America. The Asian continent is the cradle of ancient civilisations with parallel development patterns in technical, social and political structures. The impact of colonial expansion was felt throughout the area, as the Asian-Pacific region (with the exception of Japan and to a lesser extent, Thailand) fell under European or American influence. This contact has left marks on the area. The region has been the theatre of many wars, some localised, some generalised. The social fabric of China, as well as Korea, Malaysia, Kampuchea, Vietnam and Taiwan has been radically altered through deliberate political action or upon contact with Western industrial nations. There are numerous political conflicts in the area, even wars.

The Pacific Basin has been defined in various ways. The broadest sense is geographical: it is that collection of nations washed by the Pacific Ocean, including North and South America, the Asian continent and the island states east and north of Indonesia. The more widely used but restrictive sense of the term 'Pacific' is used in the Asia-Pacific concept. This groups together the market economy nations on the Pacific slope of the Asian continent, and the island states on the Asian side of the Pacific. Normally, the bulk of Latin American states are left out of this definition, as are the independent South Pacific island states, and the European nations still in the Pacific region (Great Britain, Portugal and France).

The notion of a Pacific 'community' is more in the nature of a state of mind than a concrete economic or geographic framework. Figures on growing intra-region trade and investment are used to witness to the need for a more coordinated approach to issues. Yet the problems remain unsolved: is there a real need to form a community? If so, how can real links be forged? How can awareness of shared interests be increased in an area that has differing major language groups, social and political structures, and little sense of shared common history?

B. Interest in the Concept

The concept of economic cooperation in the Asian-Pacific region has received a great deal of attention in the past fifteen years. The number of books, articles and research proposals that in some way touch upon this notion now surpasses 800 titles. Under the leadership of Prime Minister Ohira, the Japanese government sponsored an advisory study of the concept in 1979[1]; the Australian government has been active in promoting conferences and research in the area of regional economic cooperation[2]. A strong lobby group exists in the United States Congress which makes known the position of advocates of Pacific Basin integration to the legislative bodies in Washington[3]. In some developing countries of the Pacific region, there is considerable semi-official support for the concept, especially by the Government of Thailand[4]. The Economic and Social Commission of Asia and the Pacific has a large research project devoted to the economic aspects of the

1. Okita, S.(Ed.) Report on the Pacific Basin Cooperation Concept, Tokyo, 1980. The report contains the findings of a Pacific Basin Cooperation Study Group set up by the government to study the possibilities of a new regional organisation in the Pacific. It also attempts to identify common interests for Japan and other Pacific nations.

2. See the results of the Canberra Conference sponsored by the Australian government in September 1980, in Crawford, J. Pacific Economic Cooperation: Suggestions for Action, Singapore, 1980.

3. See the position paper presented to the Committee on Foreign Relations of the United States Senate: Drysdale, P. and Patrick, H. An Asian-Pacific Regional Economic Organisation: An Exploratory Paper, Washington, 1979 and a series of position papers presented to the Joint Economic Committee of the Congress of the United States: Pacific Basin Interdependencies: A Compendium of Papers Submitted to the Joint Economic Committee of the United States Congress, Washington, June 1981.

4. Thanat Khoman, presently Deputy Prime Minister of Thailand, suggested that OECD nations of the region should propose a similar organisation in the Pacific Basin (1977). In June 1982, the Thai government hosted a conference on Pacific Cooperation with the ESCAP.

question. Mexico and Chile have been particularly active in participating in discussions on a non-official basis[1].

Advocates of a more concrete form of community in the region point to increasing interdependence in trade, investment and human resource development and to the apparent community of economic aspirations for the future[2]. The record of the NICs in the region, the potential markets in South East Asia and China, and the absence of insurmountable infrastructural barriers to development mean that arguments in favour of more intense regional cooperation are not unpersuasive. Proponents of active, institutional Pacific Basin cooperation look for a "Century of the Pacific" as the motor of world economic development in the 21st century.

However, when notions of a shared destiny among the nations of the rim have been promoted in the past as a means of securing greater economic benefits for the area, they have been perceived by many of the non-industrial nations of the Pacific as basically political structures, and not economic ones created for the mutual benefit of the nations in the region. The history of failures of regional cooperation efforts in the area has left markedly sceptical attitudes on the part of South East Asian nations in particular[3]. Moreover, some critics even see plans to integrate the Pacific area as an effort to generate strategic and political structures rather than purely economic ones[4]. In evaluating the arguments for "community" in the Pacific, it is important also to consider the negative associations which this concept has in the region, as they often colour discussions of potential mutual interests.

---

1. In Chile, the Instituto de Estudios Internacionales de la Universidad de Chile organised a conference on Pacific Cooperation in October 1979, on Easter Island. There were numerous Latin American presentations. See published papers in La Comunidad del Pacifico en Perspectiva, Fr. Orrega Vicuna (Ed.), Santiago, 1979.

2. Kojima, K. "Economic Cooperation in a Pacific Community", The Japan Institute of International Affairs, Tokyo, 1980, p.9.

3. A recent criticism can be found in Leng Chuan Ong "A New Co-Prosperity Sphere", Asia Pacific Community, Vol. 9, no. 5, Summer 1979, pp.65-69.

4. For a Soviet view see S. Nikonov "A New Pacific Alliance in the Offing?", Far Eastern Affairs, Moscow, 1980, no. 3, pp.165-171.

C. Historical Background of the Concept

The complementary concept of Pan-Asian cooperation was born in the early part of the twentieth century, and although it reflects a very different form of cooperation, it stands as the historical precedent for much of what is now being discussed[1]. In this context, Morinosuke Kajima, a businessman and politician (LDP) in Japan, raised the possibility of a Pan-Pacific Community. Although this concept was a forerunner of Pan-Pacific cooperation, it was based less on economic realities than historical destinies, and in a later book published on the concept, it became clear that the 'union' of Asian countries was not backed by solid political support[2]. Kajima's scheme proposed an Asia Development Fund on the principle of the Marshall Plan.

Proposals for a Pacific Basin 'community' were first developed in the 1960s. Since that time, the idea has been debated continually in numerous publications and international conferences. It is, however, not a concept with a linear evolution, but rather a network of associated ideas being developed at the same time in different national contexts. The international conferences that have been held to discuss the idea are really nodal points in the evolution of the concept, as they represent the state of the art and future directions to be taken to create awareness of the need for institutions.

The three professional groups that have been most active in promoting the idea are university professors (including Crawford and Drysdale in Australia, Krause and Patrick in the United States, Kojima in Japan), politicians (Prime Minister Ohira in Japan, Prime Minister Fraser in Australia, Deputy Prime Minister Khoman in Thailand and Senator W. Roth in the United States) and leading businessmen (through the Pacific Basin Economic Council, a forum of over 400 leaders in industry, banking and service sectors). Although there is a flourishing activity in academic research devoted to the concept, there seems to be a more prudent "Let's wait and see" attitude of politicians in recent times as to the creation of an institutional framework for Pacific Basin associations.

In 1962, prominent economists in Japan began turning their attention to the question. Japanese interest was first demonstrated by the work of Dr. Saburo Okita and Professor Kioushi Kojima of the Hitosubashi University of Tokyo. Both

---

1. See Hoon-Mok Chung, "Economic Integration in the Pacific Basin: A Historical Review" in Han Sung-Joo (Ed.) Community Building in the Pacific Region: Issues and Opportunities.

2. Morinosuke Kajima, The Road to Pan-Asia, Tokyo 1973. For an account of the early Kajima approach to Pan-Asianism, see Tessa Morris-Suzuki, "Japan and the Pacific Basin Community", The World Today, December 1981, pp.454-61.

undertook studies on the concept of a regional cooperation institution in the Pacific area. In 1965, the Japanese Ministry of Finance sponsored a series of lectures on financial cooperation in the region, and future development possibilities.

K. Kojima was the first to make a concrete proposal for an institutional framework for the concept in 1965, when he presented his plan for a "Pacific Free Trade Area" (PAFTA), which would include the United States, Japan, Canada, Australia and New Zealand[1]. This proposal was one of the important steps in the development of the idea. Kojima later suggested a series of international regional conferences - the Pacific Trade and Development Conferences (PAFTAD). There have been thirteen so far (1983). These conferences have received official support from the Japanese Foreign Affairs Ministry[2]. Later, Japanese government officials gave tacit

---

1. Kojima raised this issue in a conference at the Japan Economic Research Centre in 1965; it was followed by a more extensive proposal made to the first Pacific Trade and Development (PAFTAD) Conference in January 1968.

2. The PAFTAD conferences are the principal forum for discussion of the Pacific Economic Cooperation idea. They gather together, at regular intervals, policy makers, government officials and private sector businessmen as well as academics, and address problems of economic cooperation both for the developed countries of the region and the developing countries. The first PAFTAD Conference was held in Tokyo in 1968; the second in Honolulu in 1969. Both addressed the problem of Pacific Free Trade Area structures. The third conference was held in Sydney in 1970 and discussed direct foreign investment in Asia and the Pacific; the fourth conference was held in Ottawa in 1971, and addressed the problems of obstacles to trade in the Pacific area. The fifth conference was held in Tokyo in 1973, and dealt with the problem of structural adjustment in Asia-Pacific trade. The sixth conference, held in Mexico City in 1974, discussed technology transfer in Pacific Economic Development; the seventh conference met in Auckland in 1975 and discussed the relations between large and small countries and the implications for Pacific economic cooperation. The eighth conference was organised in Thailand in 1976 and focussed on trade and emoployment for Asian developing countries. The ninth conference on mineral resources was held in San Francisco in 1977. The tenth conference was organised in Canberra in 1979 and addressed the problem of ASEAN and its relationship to the changing Pacific region. The 11th PAFTAD conference, held in Seoul in 1980, dealt with the advanced developing countries. Canada hosted the 12th conference in Vancouver in 1981 (renewable resources of Pacific Area). The 13th conference was organised in Manila in January 1983 (energy and structural change in the Pacific area).

support to a more expanded role for Japan in the regional economic scene. This met with a certain reticence among the developing countries of the region[1].

In the same year (1967), the Pacific Basin Economic Council (PBEC), a private initiative on the part of bankers, businessmen and leaders in industry from industrial and developing countries, was organised. The membership is currently about 400 leaders from the five OECD countries of the region, and some developing countries. The goals of the organisation were to create a forum in which the commercial relations of the region could be discussed and debated, and cooperative schemes developed. This private initiative has been very important in promoting the concept in government circles around the Pacific, as well as acting as a catalyst at the national level for stirring interest in the concept[2].

The 1970s brought a heightened governmental interest among the industrial countries of the Pacific. The rapid growth of the newly-industrialised countries of the region, the first successes of the Association of South-East Asian Nations (ASEAN, created in 1968), the promise of greater Japanese growth combined with the relative withdrawal of some of the industrial countries of the region, served as a motor for interest. During this period, the work of Lawrence Krause of the Brookings Institution in Washington DC and K. Kojima in Tokyo led the way to seeing new evidence for pan-Pacific cooperation: this cooperation was already taking place on a private basis, through the work of multinational corporations, banks and the PBEC, and a need was gradually perceived to coordinate this cooperation in an institutional form.

1978 proved to be the watershed year for the concept. After a series of meetings, both in Asia and in the industrialised countries, Senator John Glenn of the United States Senate proposed that the Congressional Research Service provide an evaluation of the concept of an economic zone in the Pacific region. The result of that proposal was published in the form of a report to the Congress of the United States. The authors, Hugh Patrick of Yale University and Peter Drysdale of the National University of Australia, put forward the suggestion that an organisation should be formed in the region to promote trade and development. This new organisation, called the Organisation for Pacific Trade and Development (OPTAD), would essentially be a forum for discussion among member states; it would lead later to a community of nations

---

1. See for example: Ghazali Bin Shefie, "Toward a Pacific Basin Community: A Malaysian Perception" in New Foundations for Asian and Pacific Security, Joyce E. Larsen (Ed.), 1980.

2. A synoptic table of existing organisations, their respective membership and functions is shown on p.65 of Annex 2.

with economic ties[1]. The OPTAD was to include the five OECD nations of the region, the five ASEAN countries and South Korea; there would be special arrangements for the Pacific Island States, Taiwan and Hong Kong. The organisation itself would resemble the OECD, but with a much smaller secretariat. Special task forces would convene for sectoral economic issues. Regional problems would be handled in a similar manner. Lawrence Krause presented a more detailed view of this type of organisation in a later publication[2].

Interest in the concept in the United States remained (and remains) principally academic. However, the trends toward liberalisation in trade throughout the world, and the growing interest in the Pacific (including the People's Republic of China), have provided new incentives for lobby and interest groups to continue their efforts.

In September 1979, an unofficial mission left the United States to visit the countries in South East Asia and ascertain the level of interest in the concept. The cautious reception of this mission in many countries led the government in Washington to leave the initiative of such an organisation to other nations. The consensus was that existing organisations, at national and the international levels would be capable of providing the needed cooperation. The promotion of a new global organisation was seen as being premature.

By this time, Prime Minister Ohira of Japan had announced his support for more cooperation in the Pacific region. A private study group of quasi-official status was set up to examine the problems of Pacific Basin cooperation from a Japanese viewpoint and make recommendations[3]. Saburo Okita was asked to act as chairman of a group of distinguished Japanese businessmen, academics and government officials. In 1980, a final report was published. Although no specific recommendations were made, and no structure as concrete as the OPTAD proposal was suggested, the report did endorse increased

---

1. "Evaluation of a Proposed Asian-Pacific Regional Economic Organization" Congressional Research Service, Library of Congress, 1979, in An Asian-Pacific Regional Economic Organization: An Exploratory Concept Paper prepared for the Committee on Foreign Relations, United States Senate, Washington, Government Printing Office.

2. Krause, Lawrence, "The Pacific Economy in an Interdependent World: A New Institution for the Pacific Basin" in Pacific Economic Cooperation: Suggestions for Action, edited by Sir John Crawford, Selangor, Malaysia, 1981.

3. The Pacific Basin Cooperation Study Group was set up in 1979; they published an interim report in November 1979 and a final report in May 1980.

efforts at cooperation. The group laid particular stress on social-cultural interdependences as well as on the specific role Japan must play in the economic future of East Asia[1].

The Australian Prime Minister, Malcolm Fraser, also took an active interest in the concept. Both he and Prime Minister Ohira sponsored an unofficial conference on the Pacific Basin cooperation concept in Canberra, Australia[2]. Three other important conferences were held from 1979 through 1980 in Chile, Indonesia, and Japan. With high-level participation from both the government sector and the private sector, the proceedings of these conferences present the major positions of many private and public officials.

A Thai initiative resulted in a conference being organised in Bangkok at the ESCAP in June 1982, where experts met to discuss concrete steps for advancing a Pacific Basin institutional framework[3]. Many of the same advocates, both from the public and private sectors, participated. The decision was taken to give a more structured format to discussion of Pacific Basin cooperation, and a steering committee for the next meeting (end of 1983, Indonesia) and three task forces (trade and manufacturing, primary commodities, transfer of technology), were established. The work of task forces, financed by institutions in Japan, Thailand, and South Korea, will focus on concrete recommendations for the creation of institutional frameworks of cooperation in the region.

These conferences, and more especially the Canberra conference, engendered a certain reticence. The watch-word became 'hasten slowly' towards institutional organisation. Requests came for more studies on the interdependences of the region. The Canberra Conference urged the creation of a 'Pacific Cooperation Committee', an informal, non-official organisation which would provide a mechanism for the exchange of information among the nations of the Pacific Basin and more especially provide sectoral information in the areas of trade, energy, marine resources and transportation.

---

1. Report on the Pacific Basin Cooperation Concept, Tokyo, 1980. See especially pp. 17-23, 41-45, and 49 of the report.

2. The results of the Canberra Conference were published in Crawford, J. and Seow, G., Pacific Economic Cooperation: Suggestions for Action, Singapore, 1981.

3. A report on this conference is given in Annex 2.

It also became clear that the involvement of ASEAN as a group was going to be a significant factor in creating any regional organisation. The participants from the ASEAN countries - with the possible exception of Thailand - saw little reason to move towards a larger structure of economic cooperation in the region. Such a move was perceived as too quick a step towards an international organisation benefitting the industrial countries of the region without providing clear advantages for the ASEAN.

Present Attitudes

The concept of Pacific Economic Cooperation has received attention from virtually all the nations that border the Pacific, and from many who do not. The industrial nations, including Japan, the United States, Canada, New Zealand and Australia have strong advocates in university, research and business circles; the official government positions in these countries are generally more cautious. The Pacific Basin Economic Council has national chapters in many of the Pacific countries, and these powerful interest groups promote discussion on the issues within national borders. They also help organise and disseminate research projects and statistical compendia which attempt to demonstrate interdependence within the region.[1] The Pan Pacific Community Association, organised in 1980 with headquarters in Washington DC acts as a relay of information and ideas to the American government and general public;[2] the Canadian government has given support to the creation of a Canada Foundation for Asia and the Pacific, and in a recent meeting a committee was named to direct the work of the Foundation.[3] In Japan, the Japan

---

1. See for instance, the Pacific Economic Community Statistics produced by the Japan National Committee of the Pacific Basin Economic Council in 1982.

2. In the spring of 1981, the Pan Pacific Community Association began publishing a Pacific Community Newsletter which acts as a means of announcing Pacific-related activities and coordinating information about research publications in the field of economic cooperation.

3. The Secretary of State for External Affairs in Canada requested a feasibility study of establishing a Canada Foundation for Asia and the Pacific in 1981. The recommendations were published in November 1982, calling for the creation of the foundation with contributions from the Federal Government of $20 million over the next three years. The territorial and provincial governments have been asked to match this sum. The study, signed by John Bruk, recommends that Canada look to the future in the Pacific area: "One of the first tasks we must do then to meet the challenge is shift our consciousness away from its historic Euro-centric focus" in Asian Pacific Foundation: A Study prepared for the Secretary of State for External Affairs, Vancouver, 1982.

Institute of International Affairs, under the chairmanship of Mr. Saburo Okita, organised a Special Committee on Pacific Cooperation (SCPC) in 1980. Among the developing countries of the region, the Centre for Strategic and International Studies (CSIS) has hosted a joint research team from the ASEAN nations which has set up an ASEAN Pacific Cooperation Committee (ASEAN-PCC). This committee will act as a relay of information and a lobby group to public and private sector groups within the region. In Korea, a Korean Committee for Pacific Cooperation was established in 1981 to coordinate activities in South Korea and to analyse the proposals for more intensive economic cooperation in the region. The Korea Development Institute hosts the secretariat of the Committee.

Official reactions among government leaders are still cautious. Korean President Chun Doo Hwan recently called for a Pacific Summit to discuss the concept in official government circles[1]. Prime Minister Trudeau's visit to Tokyo in early January, 1983 also focused on prospects for development of the Asia-Pacific area[2]. Prime Minister Nakasone's recent speech to the Asia Society in New York also echoes strong interest in developing the concept of closer economic cooperation in the Pacific.[3] In Europe, there have been important government initiatives notably in France, to understand more fully the concept and to explore it

---

1. President Chun's speech to the National Assembly on New Year's Day, 1983 included the following statement: "There is no doubt that the Pacific summit that I propose will serve as the locomotive for a system of regional cooperation and thus diplomatic efforts will be stepped up to obtain understanding and support from the major Pacific nations with a view to realizing the proposed summit at an early date."

2. "I have placed before Japan the case for creating a relationship between Japan and Canada which rejects an emphasis on narrow, short-term interests, in favour of a long-term and wide-ranging partnership." Speech to 600 Canadian and Japanese businessmen January 18, 1983, Tokyo.

3. In an address delivered to the Japan Society of the United States on 31 May, 1983, Prime Minister Nakasone made the following remark: "At the same time, I harbor a dream that the United States, Japan, the ASEAN countries, Australia, New Zealand, Canada, and all of the other countries bordering the Pacific Ocean can come together to create a new economic and cultural sphere in the twenty-first century."

further.(1) The general tone, however, of government
officials is to wait for more concrete steps to be taken in the
private sector before moving towards an official position on an
institutional structure; in point of fact, economic
cooperation already exists at the private level. It is yet to
be seen whether this will generate a greater official interest.

D.   Institutional Schemes

Forms of Cooperation

      "In the past, suggestions as to the form of an
organisation in the Pacific Basin have been varied. They range
from private business-oriented organisations to an exclusively
inter-governmental organisation. Nine major types of
organisation have been proposed:

      a)   An institutional arrangement much like that
      which exists at present, with private organisations in
      the Pacific Basin forming the locus of discussion of
      Pacific Basin economic issues, following sui generis
      agendas such as the Pacific Basin Economic Council
      (PBEC) for business leaders and the Pacific Trade and
      Development Conference (PAFTAD) for academics.

      b)   An arrangement in which various research and
      business organisations maintain formal ties. Forming a
      net over the Pacific Basin, they could monitor
      developments and, through conferences and publications,
      publicise the region's problems and propose solutions.
      A strictly private-side venture, this kind of
      organisation would be informal, as is the newly formed
      Pan Pacific Community Association.

      c)   A 'Trilateral Commission' for the Pacific
      Basin; a 'Pacific Commission', composed of prominent
      individuals who act in their private capacity and
      sponsor research and hold closed meetings on Pacific
      Basin issues.

      d)   An 'open' Pacific Commission where meetings
      would be public and the group would organise congresses
      and economic policy meetings for the sake of discussion
      and publicity.

---

1. In June 1982, the French Government held a closed seminar in
   Paris gathering together French ambassadors from the Pacific
   region to discuss closer French economic ties with the
   zone. President Mitterand's closing statement at the end of
   the seminar emphasized the need for France to follow more
   closely developments in the Pacific.

Moving more toward the governmental and formal side, there are other possibilities:

e)   The Pacific Basin countries could choose to deal with economic problems as they arise, creating more or less _ad hoc_ inter-government commissions to study issues and make non-binding policy recommendations.

f)   An intergovernmental organisation with a loose mandate and no responsibility other than to serve as an informational clearing house; it would provide a basis for regular consultative, multilateral meetings (type OPTAD).

g)   An intergovernmental organisation, charged both with being a consultative mechanism and with the task of implementing certain economic policy measures - such as lowering trade barriers throughout the Pacific, within the GATT and MFN framework. This would be a 'passively discriminatory' organisation, in that distinctly different laws or actions would not be applied on the basis of regional membership.

h)   A highly formal inter-governmental organisation with wide-ranging economic authority, having as its goal some type of economic unification of the Pacific Basin. This could be a "Common Market" of the Pacific."[1]

Membership in a Community

The establishment of a Pacific Basin community has been at the heart of proposals for cooperation in the region. The three criteria advanced so far in the debate are geographic, economic and political structures within the region.

The call for more regional cooperation on a purely geographical basis is limited. All proponents see the five OECD countries of the region belonging to the community, but the geographic argument then tilts to the Asian side: the ASEAN is seen as a key partner, as are the other NICs (South Korea, Taiwan, Hong Kong). The role of the People's Republic of China is yet to be clarified, as is the role of the

---

1. L. Krause, "Pacific Basin Co-operation", Draft Paper, Brookings Institution, August 1980.

socialist republics in South East Asia[1].

The arguments for reinforcing the links of the ASEAN and the industrial countries on the basis of growing economic interdependence are not generally accepted within the ASEAN. Critics feel that even if growing interdependence can be demonstrated, there is no assurance that a new organisation would increase regional links that are already there. ASEAN itself, a relatively young organisation, might find its interests swamped in a larger regional body just at the time when the five-country association was beginning to bear fruit[2].

The particular status of Hong Kong and Taiwan will pose undoubted problems to an eventual membership. This political problem, essentially to be resolved with the People's Republic of China, would have to be solved before steps were taken to associate the two to a regional body.

The centrally planned economies of the region might wish to play a role as observers rather than members. ASEAN itself appears to be interested in associating Vietnam more closely with economic efforts in the region, and it has also been suggested that the recent 'rapprochement' between North and South Korea could be a sign of future collaboration in a regional body.

---

1. See especially the ESCAP document DP/EGAPEC/3 prepared by Masahiko Ebashi entitled "The Role of China in the Economic Interdependence of ASEAN and the Pacific"; also relevant to the role of the People's Republic of China is the article of Hugh Patrick "US-Chinese Economic Relations in the Asian-Pacific Context" in The World Economy, June 1981. See also R. Cline, "The Communist Five and the Capitalist Ten Socio-Economic Systems in Asia", in The Journal of East-Asian Affairs, Vol.II, No.1, 1982.

2. Lee, Poh Ping, "The Pacific Community: A View of the Malaysian Study Group", The Pacific Community Concept: Views from Eight Nations. The JCIE Papers, no.1, Tokyo, 1980. An even more sceptical view, presented in a semi-official manner, is Tan Sri in Ghazali Bin Shafie "Toward a Pacific Basin Community: A Malaysian Perception" in Larsen, J. (Ed.) New Foundations for Asian and Pacific Security. The author who was Minister of Home Affairs at the time (1980) feels that the major interests of the industrial countries in the area are strategic "in effect a recycling of a Pacific 'containment' scenario". He favours very gradual association and evolution towards a consultative body.

As for the Latin American nations, no serious effort has yet been made to interest government officials throughout the area in the idea. For the moment, Chile and Mexico have been the most active in research and discussion[1].

Private sector involvement is an important factor in the success of an eventual community organisation, and it already forms the solid base for much of the existing initiatives[2].

Membership will certainly be the most debated question should concrete steps be taken to organise a community. Will all the powers that have possessions in the area be called upon to participate (notably France, Great Britain and Portugal), what type of criteria will be used to include or exclude nations that are not directly 'interdependent' at the present? In any event, the possibility must be left open for associations of different natures.

Consensus now exists that leadership for an eventual community should not be assumed by an industrial power of the region[3]. Most advocates see the role of the ASEAN as crucial in determining the success of any venture. Yet for the moment, ASEAN has been hesitant to compromise its own specificity in proposing a new framework. Although leadership must at least be shared with the developing nations of the region, it is also essential that the industrial nations take an active part in the organisation and see it as a 'mutual interest'. So far the initiative for the development of the concept has come from individuals in Japan, in the United States, Australia and to some extent Thailand.

---

1. See especially Vicuna, F., _La Comunidad del Pacifico en Perspectiva_, (two volumes) Instituto de Estudios Internacionales de la Universidad de Chile, Santiago, 1979.

2. See for example the report of the PBEC Hong Kong Meeting (1981).

3. See for example Kojima, K., "Economic Cooperation in a Pacific Community", paper presented to the Pacific Community Lecture series, East-West Center, Hawaii, 1980.

E.   Interdependences in the Region

The argument of a de facto community from existing economic interdependence is often cited. Lawrence Krause was the first to point out the three interrelated economic trends in the region: the growing economic importance of Japan, the essential motors for world economic recovery in the advanced developing countries of the region, and the decline in growth rates in Western Europe[1]. Yet the economic realities also mask political differences, and it is not certain that the two poles of interest in international cooperation - economic and political - are easily reconciliable in an international organisation that contains the industrial powers of the area as well as the developing nations[2]. Krause argues in another context that independent government action in the region has been harmful to overall regional development, and it is necessary to manage the interdependences from a central organisational point. The growing trends in protectionism, both in Europe and in the United States, were also advanced as reasons for developing a regional organisation that would handle multilateral trade issues. No existing international body was believed to have the necessary mandate to carry out the variety of tasks within the Pacific region, and it was felt that where some global negotiations had failed, a new regional body could take them up with greater success[3].

---

1. Krause, L., Economic Integration in the Pacific Basin, Washington, 1980, and in "The Pacific Economy in an Interdependent World - A New Institution for the Pacific Basin", paper delivered at the University of Washington, Seattle, October 1978, pp.8-11.

2. "Interdependence, however, creates policy problems....It is generally believed that increased economic interdependence reduces the potency of national policies...it concerns the problem of how to organise international economic relations so as to adapt the system of these relations to the fact of interdependence. The central theme of international relations today is still concerned with the problem of how to keep the manifold gains from extensive economic transactions while at the same time preserving the freedom for each nation to pursue its legitimate economic and social objectives." Hadi Soesastro, "Economic Relations in the Asia Pacific Area", Indonesian Quarterly VII: 4 (October 1979), p.28.

3. See Krause, Economic Interaction, opus cit. "Dealing with Change" p.243 ff. Millar, J.B., "A Pacific Economic Community: Problems and Possibilities", in Asia Pacific Community, no.8, pp.12-20. Millar deals with the political aspects of the proposed community, pointing out the fact that national policies in the area of employment, income and long-term investment might not be compatible with a regional level body that integrated and harmonised policies for the Pacific.

Australian advocates have examined the trends of economic development in the region, and have looked carefully at the structural adjustments that will be necessary in the future industrial development of the Pacific, as well as complementary resources of Japan, Mexico and China. Trade and trade trends for Australia remain for the proponents a primary argument for more regional cooperation[1].

Proponents and detractors of the concept of Pacific Basin integration have amply demonstrated the diversity of the region in cultural, historical and political terms[2]. The constitution of a "community" over vast spaces and in the diversity of cultures is still much debated. On a purely geographical level, the region encompasses more than half the territory of the world, if we include centrally-planned economies on the Pacific rim.

The principal characteristic of development in the NICs and other LDCs of the region is their continuous, strong growth rates over the past ten years. There is also evidence of strong commercial activity, especially in the industrial sectors (see Annex 1). The flow of commercial goods in the region mainly reflects the trade of the industrial countries of the region among themselves. Confirmed economic growth in the region will require large and growing forms of capital investment, either from capital formation within the region, and capital import, including capital from bilateral and multilateral organisations outside the region. Developing nations of the region need better investment possibilities within their own economies and the general policy framework for sustained development in cooperation with their principal commercial partners, most of whom are within the Pacific region itself. Since 1973, the industrial countries of the area have had much slower growth rates, due in part to the price shocks of oil. These countries have a definite interest in expanding their exports in the burgeoning markets of the Pacific; it is also a region that has high return rates for investment, and this latter type of flow can provide the motor for much of the growth in the area, whether in the form of joint ventures, new forms of investment or classical forms.

---

1. Whitlam, E.G., A Pacific Community, Cambridge, Massachusetts, 1981. See especially "Resources of the Pacific" Chapter 1. In the second chapter, "Western Pacific Trade", there is a presentation of growing interdependencies in the region. Gough Whitlam was Prime Minister of Australia from 1972-75. See also Drysdale, P., "Australia and the Pacific Economic Community" in Crawford, Pacific Economic Cooperation: Suggestions for Action, pp.83-87.

2. See for example: Mahatir Bin Mohamal, Datuk Seri, "Tak Kenal Maka Tak Cinta" in Asia-Pacific in the 1980s: Towards Greater Symmetry in Interdependence, CSIS, Jakarta, 1980.

F. The North-South Framework

Some of the proponents for the Pacific Basin framework have argued that North-South issues can be treated more coherently if handled on a regional basis. The value of treating such international issues in a multilateral institution, which is not dispersed over five continents, has been underlined.

The 'south' in the framework would essentially be the ASEAN nations, the People's Republic of China, and the Latin American states and Pacific Island states, should they participate. The fact that ASEAN itself is already a relatively successful policy forum for the five countries of the region would make it an excellent representative of the interests of developing nations in the region. As the NICs of the area would also be included in an eventual organisation, the trilateral discussions that could take place among the developing countries, the NICs and the industrial countries would present the possibilities for a 'mini-dialogue' in the region. The critics of this point of view feel that the establishment of such a framework might detract from the solidarity stance of developing countries of the region, and indicate a move away from global negotiations.

The Pacific Basin framework can be seen as an effective approach to the North-South question, and this for several reasons. Regional solidarity, even though vague, might be more intense than disperate, global affinities with African and Latin American developing countries. Regional efforts at economic cooperation, more easily realised in smaller frameworks, can provide initiatives and act as a motor for larger global negotiations. The example of the Lomé II Convention as an arrangement for regional cooperation is often cited as a successful framework within which North-South issues are approached multilaterally[1].

The mechanics of North-South interface might include various kinds of aid, direct foreign investment and other capital flows[2], the transfer of technology and the import of input goods which could not be provided at all, or only at

---

1. Kojima, "A New Capitalism for a New International Economic Order", Hitotsubashi Journal of Economics, Tokyo, Vol.22, N.1, June 1981, p.7.

2. Identifying the balance of payments problem as one of the major obstacles to development, Professor Kojima has proposed a regional fund that would automatically equilibrate the balance of payment of countries running a surplus or a deficit. Economic Cooperation in a Pacific Community, The Japan Institute of International Affairs, Tokyo, 1980.

much higher costs in developing countries. The process is seen
by some as an 'international complementation of national
development processes'[1], and a way to achieve at a regional
level the often called-for "New International Economic Order".

        The Pacific Island states pose special problems for
economic cooperation.[2] They are, in many ways, the most
underdeveloped countries in the region. They are also
dependent upon concessional aid flows from Australia and New
Zealand in particular. The recent independence of these states
has engendered a sense of wanting to exercise that independence
before entering into a new economic cooperation scheme that
might eventually become an economic union. A significant
amount of work is being carried out on Pacific Island states
and their economic needs by institutions in Australia, New
Zealand and the United States.

---

1. English, E., "Economic Prospects for the Asia-Pacific Region in
   the 1980s" in Asia-Pacific in the 1980s: Towards Greater
   Symmetry in Economic Interdependence, CSIS, Jakarta, 1980;
   Kitamura, H., "The Case for Asian-Pacific Regionalism: Regional
   and Sub-Regional Approaches to Multilateralism", paper
   presented to the meeting of the Association of Asian Studies,
   Toronto, Canada, mimeo. For a critical view of the
   possibilities from the ASEAN point of view, see Sicat, G., "The
   ASEAN and the Pacific Region", lecture to the East-West Center,
   Honolulu, July 1980, mimeo.

2. See the contribution of Nao Nawalowalo, "Pacific Basin
   Co-operation: A View From the Pacific Islands" in Crawford,
   op.cit., p.181. The Pacific Island states include the Cook
   Islands, Fiji, Kiribati, Nauru, Niue, Papua New Guinea, Solomon
   Islands, Tonga, Tuvali, Vanuatu and Western Samoa. There is
   also concern among the island states for the degree of nuclear
   and atomic testing in the South Pacific, an element that has
   caused friction with certain industrial countries. The
   East-West Center in Hawaii has an on-going Pacific Islands
   project, and there is a great deal of official interest in the
   evolution of these states in government circles in Australia
   and New Zealand.

II.   SECTORAL ISSUES

A.   Trade

The management of trade interdependences is the most often cited argument for the organisation of Pacific-based association of free market economies. Certain proponents have emphasised the necessity of increased multilateral negotiations in the region in order to avoid "national economic policies that are harmful to other free market economies within the zone"[1].   Krause cites such unsuccessful policies as the US embargo on soybeans in 1973 (affecting Japan), Japan's import quotas on silk (affecting Korea), Korea's "beggar thy neighbour" devaluation in 1974 (affecting Taiwan and other countries), Thailand's rice export restrictions in 1972-1973 (affecting the Philippines and Indonesia), Australia's increased protection of labour-intensive manufactures[2] etc.

Figure 1   PATTERNS OF TRADE IN THE ASIA PACIFIC REGION

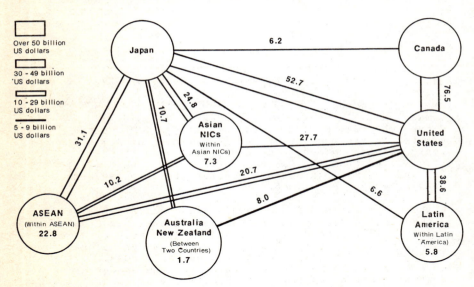

Source : Pacific Economic Community Statistics, PBEC / Japan National Committee, Tokyo, 1982.

---

1. Kojima, K., "Economic Cooperation in a Pacific Community", paper presented as part of the Pacific Community Lecture Series, East-West Center, Hawaii, 1980, mimeo.

2. Krause, Lawrence, "The Pacific Economy in an Interdependent World", mimeo, 1978.

Other authors have seen the proposals of the Group of 77 and the Non-Aligned Nations for a "New International Economic Order" in trade terms, and have found that such a structure could be approached more easily within the framework of a regional organisation than at global levels[1].

Asymmetric Interdependences

The majority of developing countries of the zone have adopted export-oriented strategies for development, as their external trade grew faster than the gross domestic product. Their trade volume now represents an important part of the GDP: between 39 per cent for the Philippines and more than 100 per cent for Hong Kong and Singapore. International trade is therefore an important motor element in development planning.

The developed countries of the region have much lower growth rates. This lower rate has been maintained, and even stimulated, by demand from developing countries, especially in the equipment and food sectors. It is partly for this reason that trade levels among countries of the region have grown steadily during the last twenty years.

Interdependence resulting from closer trade links among countries in the zone can be demonstrated by the high levels of intraregional trade among countries of the zone (see Annex 1, p.55). Indonesia leads figures with 76 per cent of its trade within the zone, and only Japan (47 per cent), Thailand (47 per cent) and the United States (44 per cent) fall under 50 per cent. Attempts have been made to characterise the intensity of trade links within the zone by using two indicators[2].

Table 1 shows that Japan's trade is as intense for imports as for exports within the Pacific zone. Trade with the United States, while remaining intense, and growing in absolute terms, is nevertheless showing signs of decrease. Japan's major trading partners are the Western Pacific nations, and this tendency has grown sharply for the period 1961-1977. United States trade flows are also heavily centred on the zone (see Table 2). These flows have, however, been in steady decline for the period 1961-1977, except for the newly-industrialised countries of the region (Hong Kong, Singapore, Taiwan, South Korea). The overall trade percentages of the US towards the Pacific have not in effect grown substantially over the past twenty years; in spite of arguments

---

1. See for example Krause, Lawrence D., "The Pacific Community Idea: Preparing for the Next Phase", paper presented at the Pacific Forum Symposium, "Strengthening Pacific Area Economic Cooperation", Makaha, Hawaii, December 1980, mimeo.

2. These two indicators are defined in Note 1, p.26.

to the contrary, it would appear that the tendency for US trade flows is actually away from the Pacific region[1]. It must be remembered, however, that "trans-Pacific patterns of relations are heavily dominated by the interactions between Japan and the US because the smaller states in East Asia and North America have done little to extend their ties with their immediate neighbours, and with their counterparts across the Pacific"[2].

TABLE 1: Intensity of Imports and Exports of Japan 1961-1977

Trading Partners of Japan	1961		1969		1977	
	m	x	m	x	m	x
Indonesia	1,9	5,6	7,4	4,8	7,4	4,5
China	0,7	0,6	2,9	3,4	3,8	3,9
Australia - New Zealand	4,0	1,5	5,3	2,2	4,9	2,7
Other countries South Asia *	3,9	6,7	3,9	4,3	4,1	2,9
Asia - rapid development **	2,3	3,7	2,4	4,7	2,3	4,1
United States	2,2	2,4	2,2	2,4	1,6	2,0
OPEC Middle East	2,8	2,0	2,9	2,0	3,4	2,2

Source: Centre d'Etudes Prospectives et d'Informations
Internationales (hereafter "CEPII"), Paris, n.d.

Note: 'm' = intensity of imports; 'x' = intensity of exports
(For a detailed explanation of these terms, see Note 1, p.26)

*   includes the Philippines, Malaysia, Thailand, Sri Lanka, Bangladesh and the smaller countries of the Asia-Pacific region.
**   this group includes South Korea, Taiwan, Hong Kong and Singapore.

1. Drysdale, P., and Patrick, H., "Evaluation of a Proposed Asian-Pacific Regional Economic Organization", An Asian-Pacific Regional Economic Organisation: An Exploratory Concept Paper, Washington, 1979.

2. Boyd, Gavin, "Transpacific Politics" in Region Building in the Pacific, Boyd, Gavin (Ed.), 1982.

TABLE 2: <u>Intensity of Imports and Exports of the United States with the Asia-Pacific zone</u>

Trading Partners of the United States	1961		1969		1977	
	m	x	m	x	m	x
Indonesia	1,0	2,3	1,2	1,7	2,2	1,3
China	0	0	0	0	0,2	0,2
Australia - New Zealand	1,0	1,0	1,1	1,5	0,6	1,8
Other countries South Asia	1,1	1,4	1,3	1,0	1,3	1,1
Asia - rapid development	0,8	1,2	2,4	1,1	2,4	1,6
Japan	2,2	2,4	2,4	2,2	2,0	1,6

Source: CEPII, Paris, n.d.

Australia and New Zealand, on the contrary, are intensifying their trade within the zone, due in some part to the entry of the United Kingdom into the European Common Market and the end of preferential Commonwealth trade links. Their trade is particularly intense with Japan, the ASEAN countries, and China (see Table 3).

TABLE 3: <u>The most intense trade links of Australia and New Zealand</u>

3a

Trading Partners of Australia and New Zealand	1969		1977	
	m	x	m	x
Australia - New Zealand *	3,1	3,1	4,7	4,7
Japan	2,2	5,3	2,7	4,9
China	0,2	3,2	0,2	4,9
Other countries South Asia	1,4	3,4	1,4	3,4
Asia - rapid development	1,7	1,2	2,6	1,7
United Kingdom	3,7	2,8	2,3	1,2
Indonesia	4,8	1,6	0,4	2,4
United States	1,5	1,1	1,8	0,6

Source: CEPII, Paris
Note: * Exchange between the two countries

The newly-industrialised nations of the zone have tried to diversify their trade links but at the same time have remained primarily Pacific trade partners (see Table 4). These have not really been able to penetrate the Japanese home market, as specialised studies have recently revealed [1], and as the decreasing value of the two indicators 'm' and 'x' shows.

TABLE 4: Trade links of newly-industrialised countries of Asia

Trading partners of NICs	1969		1977	
	m	x	m	x
China	8,8	1,6	7,9	0,5
Other countries South Asia	4,4	5,2	3,5	4,3
Indonesia	6,4	4,7	4,2	3,1
Japan	4,7	2,4	4,1	2,3
NICs of Asia	2,3	2,3	2,4	4,8
Australia - New Zealand	1,2	1,7	1,7	2,6
United States	1,1	2,4	1,6	2,4

Source: CEPII, Paris

---

1. Christian Sautter, then Director of the Centre d'Etudes Prospectives et d'Informations Internationales, defined in his article "Le Japon et l'Asie-Pacifique" (Economie et Prospective, No.4, Octobre 1980), an indicator "x" for the intensity of exports from one country to another, using the formula:

$$x = \frac{xij}{xi.} : \frac{x.j}{x..}$$

where 'xij' represents the flow of exports from country 'i' to country 'j', in US$

'xi.' represents the total amount of exports from country 'i', in US$

'x.j' represents the total amount of exports to country 'j', in US$

'x..' represents the total world export, in US$

If 'x' is greater than one, it means that exports of country 'i' are mostly oriented towards country 'j', or in other words, that exports from country 'i' to country 'j' represent a bigger part of total exports of country 'i' than the importance of country 'j' in world trade. Sautter defined in a similar way an indicator "m" for the intensity of imports of a country 'i' from a country 'j' by:

$$m = \frac{xji}{xi.} : \frac{x.j}{x..}$$

Indonesia presents a special case within the zone. It is the sole member of OPEC within the region, and its trade flows with Japan are well established, in great part due to its energy export potential (see Table 5). The growing role of ASEAN integration may well change this situation in the future, with more interlinked trade planned within the association.

TABLE 5: Trade links of Indonesia

Trading partners of Indonesia	1969		1977	
	m	x	m	x
Japan	4,8	7,4	4,5	7,4
Asia - rapid development	4,7	6,4	3,1	4,2
China	6,4	-	4,3	-
Other countries South Asia	2,4	3,1	3,1	1,0
United States	1,7	1,2	1,3	2,2
Australia - New Zealand	1,6	4,8	2,4	0,4

Source: CEPII, Paris

Without attempting to break down trade patterns according to individual products, it is possible to identify trade flows that structure trade patterns. The United States is a major exporter of agricultural products and foodstuffs, and a major importer of consumer goods. Japan's imports are principally restricted to raw materials and foodstuffs; exports are principally consumer goods, intermediary goods and capital goods. The Asian NICs export mainly consumer goods (to the US), foodstuffs (to Japan), and petroleum products. They import equipment goods (from Japan and the US), and foodstuffs (from the US).

The commodity pattern of ASEAN exports is in striking contrast to the pattern of imports. Except for Singapore, whose domestic exports are mainly manufactured goods, exports are concentrated on primary commodities, or primary- commodity-based products, although manufactured exports have been growing very rapidly and are currently standing at 25 per cent of the total exports[1]. On the import side, capital goods account for more than 60 per cent of total imports. In Thailand and the Philippines, petroleum products represent more than 30 per cent.

---

1. See for example ESCAP, Dynamics of Industrialization in the Pacific, and the Industrialization of ASEAN, note by the Secretariat, DP/EGAPEC/8, Bangkok, 24 May 1982.

Trade flows within the Asia-Pacific region have three major characteristics:

  i)   the weight of the two industrial powers of the region (Japan and the United States);
  ii) the importance of South-South trade;
  iii) the asymmetric nature of the trade patterns.

The economic power of Japan and the United States conditions their relationships with other nations within the region and many of the developing nations of the area have been reluctant to enter into an organisation that would include both industrial powers of the region and developing nations. There is a certain fear that the two giant industrial powers would dominate any such organisation[1].

There is evidence of a high level of South-South trade within the region. This trade is more equilibrated, as the partners have comparable economic weight. It is on the increase, and will probably continue so, especially within the ASEAN where trade barriers have been substantially lowered over the past 10 years. The NICs might have a larger role to play in the future, especially in substituting for industrial nations in the export of equipment goods.

The asymmetric trade relationships within the region are evidenced by the chronic trade deficits of developing countries within the zone towards Japan. Regional equilibrium is maintained, however, by the exports to the United States which absorb many of the export goods of developing nations of the region, thus providing a motor for development. This situation has, in recent years, been the focus of debate within the United States, under growing pressure of large trade deficits with the Western Pacific countries (Annex 1, p.55).

The economies of the Asia-Pacific zone are already well integrated, and there may be said to exist already a de facto economic community. However, it is ultimately in the political arena that the question of the extent and form of integration will be determined, with reference to economic evidence. The industrial countries of the Basin may well not wish to see their bilateral trade relations submerged in multilateral integration for the region, and it is not clear whether an association that established preferences and thus implied discrimination would even be in the interest of the majority of the countries in the zone, given their foreign trade-based growth strategy.

---

1. Goh, Chok Tong, "The Role of National Governments in Strengthening Economic Interdependence in the Asia-Pacific Region", Asia Pacific in the 1980s: Toward Greater Symmetry in Economic Interdependence, CSIS, Jakarta, 1980.

The major development issue for the non-OECD countries of the region, including the NICs, remains a precarious balancing act of political and economic equilibrium and a rapid increase in industrialisation. In the market economies of the region, this strategy is powered by trade growth. Yet trade growth cannot be carried out with indiscriminate goals; the optimal growth takes place with hard currency markets, and in that respect developing countries are competitors for market shares with industrial countries both inside and outside the zone[1].

Issues for Regional Cooperation

Advocates for an Asia-Pacific community put emphasis on four points:

i) Developing countries of the Asia-Pacific region have chosen an export-oriented development policy and therefore need access to large and expanding markets, as they move up to more elaborate exports that improve the terms of trade[2]. This expansion would lay the base for industrial development, subsequently permitting the area to up-grade its exports to other areas.

ii) Developed countries are experiencing lower growth rates than in the past and would therefore benefit from extended trade relations with the most dynamic economic poles of the world (the Western Pacific)[3].

iii) These two interests can be rendered compatible if industrial structural adjustment is promoted inside developed countries[4].

---

1. Nicholas, Rhondda, "ASEAN and the Pacific Community Debate: Much Ado about Something?", Asian Survey, December 1981.

2. See for example Wanandi, Jusef, "The Role of the United States in the Pacific", paper presented at the Pacific Forum Symposium, "Strengthening Pacific Area Economic Cooperation", December, 1980.

3. See for example English, H. Edward, "Canada and Pacific Opportunities", paper prepared for the 1981 meeting of the Association of Asian Studies, Toronto, Canada, mimeo.

4. Kojima, Kiyoshi, "A New Capitalism for a New International Economic Order" in Hitotsubashi Journal of Economics, Vol.22, No.1, June 1981.

iv)   This last issue could be dealt with more
successfully in a group of like-minded market-economy
nations(1).

Apart from the often called-for trade liberalisation
through a progressive "lessening" of tariff and non-tariff
barriers, national macro-economic policies might be better
coordinated. Furthermore an Asebex, equivalent in its principle
to the Stabex, could be created in order to reduce export
earnings instability.

A possible set of features for an ASEBEX is formulated in
an ESCAP Secretariat document as follows:

Commodity coverage	:	Rubber, timber, tin, sugar, coffee, palm oil, coconut oil and copra, copper, rice.
Destinations	:	Australia, Canada, China, Hong Kong, Japan, Republic of Korea, New Zealand, United States, ASEAN, other Asia-Pacific.
Compensation	:	Commodity by commodity.
Target	:	Five-year geometric moving average in current dollars, calendar year.
Eligibility threshold	:	Zero per cent.
Terms and conditions	:	Interest-free loan, drawings and repayments are automatically processed at the end of the shortfall or surplus years.

Source: ESCAP Secretariat document (unnumbered) prepared for the
conference held in Bangkok, June 3-5, 1982: "ASEAN and
Pacific Cooperation".

ESCAP also made an attempt to measure the stabilisation
effect of ASEBEX on total export earnings. This exercise shows
that the ASEBEX would have a very stabilizing effect on such
countries as Malaysia and the Philippines, a smaller effect on
Thailand, and hardly any effect on Indonesia.

1. Kitamura, Hiroshi, "The Case for Asian-Pacific Regionalism -
   Regional and Sub-Regional Approach to Multilateralism",
   mimeo., 1981.

B. Investment

      The predicted high growth rates as well as relatively low inflation rates of some of the newly-industrialised nations and of the developing countries of the Pacific region (when compared to industrial nations outside the region) offer attractive investment prospects, and this has aroused strong interest among industrial nations and OPEC countries. Growth rates that hover between 5-7 per cent in most of the countries of the East Asia region are more attractive for potential lenders than those in Latin America or Africa (cf. Annex 1, p.50), especially since the external debt of the first group is not as heavy a burden as for many other developing countries.

      During the past fifteen years, there has been a transformation of capital flow trends. Flows from private banking sources have grown more quickly than those emanating from international agencies, such as the World Bank or the Asian Development Bank (although in absolute terms, international agencies are still ahead of private sources). The Asian Development Bank financed 58 projects in 17 different countries (total: US$ 1.5 billion) in the year 1980. The majority of these loans are from soft loan funds. Within the Bank, special contribution funds are necessary each year to replenish soft loan funds. The Bank now co-finances many projects in the region with the cooperation of other international agencies (only rarely with private banking sources); 90 per cent of co-financing is with official organisations (the World Bank, the World Health Organisation, the EEC, the OPEC Fund for International Development).

      Financing is also carried out through national and multinational private corporations. The channels of this financing are either direct forms of investment or 'new forms of foreign investment', such as turn-key operations, international subcontracting, licensing agreements, management contracts, and joint ventures[1].

      Direct foreign investment constitutes a somewhat controversial form of financial cooperation, as it involves not only the transfer of capital, but simultaneously transfers of technology, marketing strategies, and management techniques. The ASEAN nations are particularly involved in this direct form of investment.

      The major investor nations in the ASEAN countries are Japan, followed by the United States, the newly-industrialised nations (Hong Kong), the European Community nations, and Australia. Japan alone accounted for more than $4 billion in 1981, or 44 per cent of the total investment figures in the region as against 25 per cent for the United States. The

---

1. The importance of such 'new forms' of investment for Korea, the Philippines, Malaysia and Singapore is shown in the forthcoming OECD Development Centre publication New Forms of International Investment in Developing Countries, by Charles Oman, et alia.

progress in Japanese investment can be measured against 1976
figures: Japan 33 per cent of investment, and the United
States 23 per cent. Together, the United States and Japan
provide more than 69 per cent of direct foreign investments in
ASEAN nations, with the exception of Singapore (47 per cent)
and Malaysia (40 per cent). American and Japanese investments
are geographically, as well as sectorially, selective: broadly
speaking, American flows are towards Singapore and the
Philippines in manufactured goods sectors (chemicals,
electronics and transport). Japanese investment is towards
Thailand and Indonesia. A break-down of American and Japanese
investments, by country within the zone, are shown on p.5 and 6
of Annex 1.

    For the host country, the problem of maintaining
national sovereignty over certain sectors remains a sensitive
issue, particularly when the level of foreign investment is
high. This is particularly acute in the ASEAN nations, where
there is at once high awareness of sub-regional interdependence
with collective future growth, and a fertile terrain for inter-
and intra-industrial specialisation in the region[1].

Prospects for Interdependence

    The importance of the credit and bond markets in South
East Asia is already apparent from regional structures. Yet
existing financial structures at the regional level are
inadequate, often rigid, and generally closed to cooperative
efforts. Thus, the Japanese authorities used to require
countries seeking to issue bonds in Japan to establish a track
record in other reputable bond markets, before permitting them
to proceed to a foreign bond issue. Many officials from
developing countries in the region stress that capital markets,
and especially stock and bond markets should be further
liberalised[2]. They argue that whereas the worldwide ratio
of total loans to total bond issues was about 2 to 1 in 1979,
or $96 billion to $40 billion, this ratio stood at 13 to 1, or
$17 billion to $1.3 billion, in the Western Pacific

---

1. See statement by Sommai Hoontrakool, then Chairman of The
   Industrial Finance Corporation of Thailand in his paper
   "Transfer of Technology and Management Know-How in Joint
   Ventures", prepared for the Symposium: "Business
   Cooperation between Asia-Pacific and Japan in the Eighties",
   held in Tokyo, 26-27 May 1980, (hereafter referred to as
   Business Cooperation Symposium).

2. As stated by Victor Macalincag, then Assistant-Minister of
   Finance (Philippines), during the Business Cooperation
   Symposium (Final Report, p.193).

Region[1]. Furthermore, if the region as a whole can provide
sufficient incentives for foreign investment, new regional
structures might be necessary to harmonise and coordinate flows
from industrial nations and other net capital exporters towards
and within the region. One such measure could be the opening
of the credit and bond markets to non-residents of the host
country (whether industrial or developing) in order to allow
investment or borrowing on the home market[2].

Recently in Japan, direct or indirect constraints have
been curtailed (such as the closing down of administrative
'caution' companies with separate administration control
exercised by government agencies, the attribution of licences
has been facilitated). Certain fiscal advantages have been
offered to foreign investors, and measures have been taken to
make it less difficult to expatriate investment gains. The
restrictions that limited foreign investment in Japanese
companies to 10 per cent of shares have now been revised (this
may now be modified with the approval of the Ministry of
Finance). The ceiling of 25 per cent for equity participation
has been modified as well in 1981.

Institutions such as the Export-Import Bank or the
Overseas Economic Cooperation Fund (Japan) have been given
official support in order to reinforce international geographic
financial cooperation. The loans and investments have been
diversified. Government measures have tried to avoid
short-term policy goals tending, for example, to equilibrate
the commercial balance or stabilise the rate of exchange; more
frequent use is made of open market policies instead of
bilateral transactions with the Central Bank.

From the point of view of the countries that borrow
funds, the situation is the exact opposite, but the imperative
remains to create liberal market possibilities and financial
infrastructures that are appropriate to needs. Rigid
investment restrictions exist in many developing countries of
the region: in Indonesia, the administrative formalities
necessary for direct investment are heavy, as permits are
necessary for every step (production, distribution, transport,
movement); in Malaysia, one third to one half of the shares of
the firm must be owned by indigenous Malays; in the
Philippines, there are important restrictions upon foreign
participation in national companies, especially those that
exploit natural resources.

---

1. Figures issued by Yusuke Kashiwagi, then President of the
   Bank of Tokyo Limited, during the Business Cooperation
   Symposium (Final Report, p.200).

2. The Pacific Basin Cooperation Study Group, Final Report on
   the Pacific Basin Cooperation Concept, Tokyo, May 19, 1980.

The financial planning of projects has become an
essential aspect[1]. The precision with which projectsand
financing must now be planned require more sophisticated
statistical and economic analysis capability in developing
countries themselves.

The role of the Asian Development Bank in the region has
grown over the years, both in terms of direct financing and in
terms of stimulating private finance[2]. The Pacific Basin
Economic Council has in the past proposed a charter of "good
conduct" (the Charter on International Investment) which would
regulate agreements for both borrowers and lenders. There have
also been recent moves to create multinational private regional
banks, such as the Private Investment Company of Asia, an
investment bank that takes minority participation in financing
public sector projects within the region.

In the area of foreign investment, it is important that
information be exchanged quickly. In the Pacific region, there
is already a relatively high degree of coordination among
banks. In ASEAN, the Asian Banking Council, which was created
in 1976, coordinates the activities of commercial banks on a
regional basis. This institution has become partly a
commercial bank on its own and partly a holding company
offering services to businessmen who are operating in other
countries of ASEAN. The Banking Council also serves as the
institution through which much of Japanese investment enters
the ASEAN region.

Developing countries are quite dependent on foreign
investment to keep their growth rate at a high level[3].
This fact has led in the past to an "investment code
war"[4]. Such competition to attract foreign investors is
obviously harmful for developing countries and the
harmonisation of foreign investment incentives would be an
important issue that could well be dealt with inside an
Asia/Pacific community.

---

1. Kojima, Kiyoshi, "A New Capitalism for a New International
   Economic Order" in Hitotsubashi Journal of Economics,
   Vol.22, No.1, June 1981.

2. Kojima, Kiyoshi, "Development-Oriented Foreign Investment
   and the Role of the ADB", Economic Office Report Series,
   No.4, ADB, April 1982.

3. As stated by Tengku Razaleigh Hamzah, Minister of Finance of
   Malaysia, in his paper "Foreign Investment and
   Industrialization of the Host Country", prepared for the
   Business Cooperation Symposium (Final Report, p.76).

4. Hoontrakool, Sommai, op.cit., p.93.

In 1981, the ASEAN created the ASEAN Finance Corporation which offers opportunities to firms in the area of capital transfers, management problems and technical assistance. This middle-level institution was created precisely to bridge the gap between the multinational financial institutions and the local-level banks and enterprises.

Recently, there has been an initiative from the Pacific Basin Economic Council Study Group on finance to create a Pacific Basin Finance Conference which would bring together private bankers in order to exchange information, organise regional meetings and special meetings with the heads of central banks in the zone. Another proposal was put forward by the Export-Import Bank of Japan: the creation of an "Asian-Pacific Bankers Club" to discuss ways and means of enhancing mutual benefits through financial and monetary cooperation. Advocates do not go so far as to propose a monetary union resembling the European Monetary System[1].

C. Energy

Energy interdependence within the region has been used as a basis for promoting closer cooperation in the Pacific. With the exception of Australia and Canada (which are able to satisfy their own needs and no more) and Malaysia and Indonesia (which are net exporters of energy resources), the other countries of the region are net importers of energy. However, the level of energy dependence, measured as the part of imported energy in the total consumption of energy, varies a great deal: 20 per cent in the United States, 58 per cent in South Korea, 60 per cent in New Zealand, 72 per cent in Taiwan, 92 per cent in Thailand and Japan, and 100 per cent in Singapore and Hong Kong[2]. This situation is not likely to change in the near future, unless massive nuclear energy campaigns are undertaken in the advanced industrial nations of the region.

---

1. As stated by Masao Fujioka, then Executive Director of the Export-Import Bank of Japan, in his paper "Expanded Financial Ties between Asia-Pacific and Japan", prepared for the Business Cooperation Symposium.

2. Figures released at the Williamsburg Conference: "Coexistence of Differing Systems in the Pacific Basin; Styles and Mechanisms for Crisis Management" held in November 1980.

Oil remains the single most important source of energy within the region, due in part to the relatively low prices over the past twenty years, the facility of storing and the rapidity of transport across great distances. Oil provides 73 per cent of the energy resources in Japan, 100 per cent in Singapore, 93 per cent in Malaysia, 77 per cent in Indonesia and 44 per cent in the United States[1].

Energy is one of the few inputs in which the region is not self-sufficient. Those countries that import oil rely upon Indonesia, Malaysia, and the People's Republic of China, who respectively exported 62, 7, and 25 million tons of oil in 1979[2]. The rest of the deficit (some 550 million tons of oil) comes from the Middle East.

One of the most important factors in Pacific region growth throughout the 1980s will be the price of crude oil as it is set in the oil market. It is increasingly a concern of the developing as well as the industrial nations of the region, to be able to meet their oil needs and ensure their supplies. The following table shows the growing importance of energy imports on the commercial balance. Energy imports also negatively affect the balance of payments through the increasing cost of freight.

---

1. Source: 1979 Yearbook of Energy Statistics.

2. Source: ibid.

Oil Imports as a Percentage of Total Imports

	1973	1974	1979	1981
Japan	17.5	34.1	34.3	38.7
Korea	6.5	14.1	15.3	24.4
Singapore	12.9	24.0	25.2	34.0
Philippines	9.3	15.8	16.9	24.5
Thailand	8.5	16.2	16.0	21.7
Malaysia	2.9	4.9	7.4	7.9
Australia	3.6	7.4	9.5	13.5
New Zealand	7.7	11.0	n.a.	n.a.

Source: IMF, International Financial Statistics, November 1980.

The strategies for energy vary greatly among the nations of the region and the strategies of the industrial countries are not those of the developing nations. Due to the balance of payment constraints, many developing nations are looking more actively to the development of domestic energy resources (such as the geothermic campaign in the Philippines, the coal campaign in China and Indonesia, or the development of offshore natural gas production in Thailand and Malaysia). The reserves in primary energy resources of the countries in the region are shown in Annex 1, p.8. As emphasised by the ESCAP Secretariat[1], it is clear that the region is well endowed with coal. As coal exploitation is more labour-intensive, its utilisation does not lead to an excessive forest depletion, and as the cost of production is competitive with the price of oil at the margin, the ESCAP Secretariat suggests that this source of energy be developed, and that more systematic explorations increase its proven reserves throughout the region. The use of coal where it is most suitable (power generation, etc.) should ease the balance of payment problems in some countries and increase regional security in energy. In the case of Indonesia,

1. ESCAP, working paper presented by the Secretariat for the fifth session of the Working Group Meeting on Energy Planning and Programming and of the Committee on Natural Resources, Energy Resources Development Series, No. 20, U.N., New York, 1979.

if coal is to be used domestically, it would increase the volume
of oil available for export. But coal can also be traded
internationally. Australia for example will in the near future
export important quantities of coal, thus increasing regional
self-sufficiency in energy.

Alternative energy resources are now being explored
regionally, such as small-scale hydro sources, and solar, wind,
tidal and biomass resources available at a relatively low
investment cost, although at quite a high investment cost per
unit of output[1]. However, in these fields small-scale
technologies have inherent limitations; they are better
described as transitional than long-term technologies[2].

Growth prospects versus consumption

Oil expenditures have been on the increase in the region
since 1974. Domestic inflation has been fed by the combination
of rising prices of crude oil and the deterioration of energy
trade balances throughout the region (with the partial exception
of Indonesia and Malaysia, which are oil producers). Economic
growth is slowing down throughout the region. Economic recovery
has been hampered in part by the energy supply situation.

Japan has in great measure overcome the adverse effects
of the second oil crisis, handling the burden on its balance of
payments by converting to a less energy-consuming industrial
structure and maintaining its export competitiveness[3].

Developing countries in the region will continue to be
adversely affected by the crude oil energy prices that caused
their terms of trade to deteriorate and negatively affected
their balance of payments. They do possess, however, advantages
over other developing countries throughout the world; they have
high potential for growth throughout the 1980s; they possess,
for the most part, an industrial structure that could allow them
to switch to less expensive energy sources in the coming
years[4]; and they could develop and use coal, lignite,
natural gas, wood, hydro and biomass sources over the coming
decade.

1. World Bank, Energy in the Developing Countries, Washington
   D.C., 1980.

2. Wad, Atul, in Proceedings of the South-East Asian Workshop
   on Energy Policy and Management, The World Bank, Washington
   D.C., 1981, p.23.

3. A good example is developed by Naoto Shinkawa in his paper
   "Energy Conservation in Japanese Industry, the case of
   Yawaka Works, Nippon Steel Corporation", Proceedings, op.cit.

4. Eguchi, Yujiro, "Energy Issues and Economic Development in
   the Pacific Countries", The Asian Club Occasional Paper, A5,
   1981.

The majority of commercial energy consumption within the region is used for the industrial and transport sectors. As industrialisation continues in the developing countries of the region, the needs in terms of energy will grow. Large-scale production plants in areas such as steel, chemicals and cement increase the energy yield in these high-consumer sectors. Yet the domestic market in most individual countries of the region cannot absorb the excess production of a larger plant. Although in favourable growth periods the excess may be exported at competitive prices, during economic stagnation these exports slacken. As a result, investment aimed at reducing energy use is slowed down.

<u>Energy Consumption/GDP Elasticity and Per Capita Energy Consumption</u>

Country	Elasticity		Per Capita Energy Consumption in Kilograms Coal Equivalent (1978)
	1970-1974	1974-1978	
Korea	0.83	0.89	1,359
Taiwan	1.07	1.69	2,202
Hong Kong	1.03	1.17	1,657
Malaysia	1.60	0.66	716
Singapore	2.58	1.23	2,461
Thailand	1.12	1.02	327
Philippines	0.89	0.99	339
Indonesia	1.05	3.79	278
Japan	0.89	0.47	3,825

Sources: 1. United Nations, <u>World Energy Supplies</u>, 1950-74 and 1973-78.
2. World Bank, <u>World Development Report</u>, 1980.

The issues facing the developing nations of the region as far as their energy policy is concerned, might be classified in two groups:

i) <u>action on the demand for energy</u>

In the short-term, in order to alleviate balance of payments problems in countries where one of the main bottlenecks for development is capital scarcity, and in times when the international financial markets seem particularly unstable, governments might want to foster energy conservation and to develop a less energy-consuming industrial structure (by cutting back, for example, on aluminium production). An efficient way to implement such a policy would be to play on energy prices, in order to give convenient signals to industrial and private consumers[1], which would incite them to reduce their consumption.

ii) <u>action on the supply of energy</u>

In the longer term, countries might try to diversify their sources of energy to increase their national energy security, by switching to domestically-available sources. However, they will probably have to study the financial rate of return of such projects in order to avoid diverting scarce capital resources from other industrial projects.

An important field for implementation of such policy measures is the transport sector, which uses a large proportion of the energy imported. Unlike the pattern followed by the industrial nations of today, where railroad expansion was the major transport infrastructural development, these nations have favoured road transport and, to a lesser extent, air transport, which are forms of transport with high energy consumption. The policy task facing developing countries is to produce incentives to reduce energy costs in the road and air sector by planning and building more effective mass transit systems with low energy needs and better sea-going low energy vessels. This policy of conversion would require action that ensures that gasoline prices reflect market prices and thus reduce consumption.

---

1. Bharier, Julian, "Pricing Energy Products", <u>Proceedings</u>, <u>op. cit</u>, p.75.

Prospects for Regional Cooperation

ESCAP studies indicate that the implementation of new policies regarding energy problems in the developing countries is often constrained by bottlenecks in the availability of capital, technology and trained manpower[1]. The development of domestic energy resources requires a long lead time and generates high financial risks. Developed and developing countries in the region might agree to cooperate more closely in order to spread this financial risk, especially for less profitable domestic energy projects (natural gas, lignite, new sources of energy).

Technologies adaptable to some countries in the region and transferable to them by those who have mastered them (for example, developing countries like Brazil) include:

- the utilisation of satellites to explore new energy fields;

- forest resource management to develop tree-farming as a source of energy[2];

- cultivation of "energy-producing" crops that maximise the alcohol yield per hectare;

- liquefaction and gasification of coal[3];

- harnessing of geothermal energy[4];

- conservation technologies.

At the same time, training institutes would be needed to increase the availability of trained manpower. One proposal to facilitate regional cooperation in these fields, put forward by the Pacific Basin Cooperation Study Group under the chairmanship of Dr. Saburo Okita, would be to set up a "Pacific Basin Resources and Energy Research Institute".

---

1. ESCAP, Energy Resources Development Series, No. 20, U.N., New York, 1979.

2. Villegas, Fernando, "Resource-based Development in the Pacific Basin", a paper prepared for the Pacific Forum Symposium: "Strengthening Pacific Area Economic Cooperation" held in December 1980.

3. The Pacific Basin Cooperation Study Group, Final Report on the Pacific Basin Cooperation Concept, May 1980, p.52.

4. Ibid.

Indonesia, Malaysia, and perhaps Thailand[1] might agree to sign long-term contracts stabilising energy prices. The setting up of joint stockpiling could conceivably also be considered. Both oil importing and oil exporting countries might seek ways to harmonize their domestic energy price systems, to foster energy conservation, and to promote fair and effective industrial competition[2].

D. Food Security

Regional management of food supplies is especially pertinent to the Asian-Pacific zone market economies[3]. Larger food stocks, improved transportation of existing supplies, methods for higher yields in rice, diversified cultivation, automated farming techniques and appropriate food technologies are all issues that could be dealt with on a regional basis.

Food security can also be seen as a regional issue in the context of North-South discussions. For most of the developing countries of the area (including the ASEAN nations), an accelerated modernisation of the agricultural sector is a long-term necessity for larger food supplies. It would also bring higher yields. This up-grading requires increased investments and larger skilled manpower pools in the agricultural sector (whether in the case of technology transfers or more modest appropriate technology implementation)[4].

In commercial terms, a better regional cooperation could lead to regular lines of supply for agricultural goods, better commercial balances for developing countries, and a more stable price structure.

---

1. Thailand is currently considering the export of liquefied natural gas (LNG) from its offshore fields.

2. Joint Economic Committee, Pacific Region Interdependencies, Washington, June 1981, p.43.

3. The OECD countries, the five ASEAN countries, Hong Kong, Taiwan, South Korea, and the South Pacific Island states.

4. Villegas, Bernardo, "Resource-based Development in the Pacific Basin", background paper prepared for the 1980 Pacific Forum Symposium, p.8.

Regional Perspectives

The nations of the Pacific Basin are in some measure agriculturally complementary. The zone comprises food exporting countries (the United States, Canada, Australia, Thailand, for cereals and meat) and food importers (Japan, South Korea, Taiwan, Indonesia, Hong Kong, Singapore, Malaysia and the Philippines) as well as nations which are net exporters of non-food agricultural products (Malaysia and Indonesia for vegetable oils and wood).

Agricultural imports represent almost 15 per cent of the total imports for Japan, and almost 70 per cent of total exported goods for New Zealand, making agricultural trading particularly intense in the zone. Although long-term projections indicate that worldwide potential demand will not be supply-constrained, it is the case that the difference between the developed nations' surplus and the developing nations' needs will also grow[1]. Food deficits will be particularly acute in South East Asia, as the following table indicates:

Gross Deficit in the Projection of Major Staples 1975-1990
(in thousands of metric tons)

	1975	1990 scenarios low growth	1990 scenarios high growth
Hong Kong & Singapore	1385	2317	2638
Indonesia	2127	5985	7656
Korea	2316	5810	6570
Malaysia	857	387	454
Philippines	276	1443	1738
Thailand	(3669) surplus	(6972)	(6771)
Total	3282	8970	12,285

Source: International Food Policy Research Institute, Washington D.C.

1. Food and Agriculture Organisation, Agriculture: Towards 2000; International Food Policy Research Institute, Food Needs of Developing Countries, Projections of Production and Consumption to 1990, Washington D.C., 1977.

In the case of Japan, the impact of new food products (principally Western meats and cereals) could have an even more dramatic effect upon the food import situation should this market become more receptive to non-traditional foods. These food needs can be satisfied in major part by intra-regional trading. Harmonisation of trade and coordination of the complementarity of traded goods could bring greater awareness of interdependence in the Pacific region, and perhaps lead to an argument for an institutional forum in which coherent patterns of self and mutual interests can be established on food security issues.

It has been argued[1] that a regional organisation, even with only consultative powers, would be in a position to foster more coherent trading patterns, assuring food needs for nations with deficits and providing stable markets for nations with large export capacity in the region. However, critics maintain that it remains to be demonstrated that a regional organisation would have greater facility in promoting more coherent management of existing inter-dependencies than bilateral or multilateral efforts to date.

The North-South Questions of Food Security

Many factors can effect a change in a country's ability to satisfy food needs: among them, bad harvests, inclement weather, too great a dependence upon one food staple which is imported from a single partner, unstable political conditions, transport prices. In the long term, the issue is a more substantial one: how to change existing techniques of production to ensure higher yields, resulting in less dependence upon outside suppliers, how to diversify food consumption patterns to take into account changes in nutritional needs with changes in labour deployment, or changes (up-grading) in consumption patterns.

Developing nations of the region depend heavily upon rice, wheat and to a lesser extent, meat and fish supplies. The predominance of rice as a base food in the region makes it imperative that stocks be available with easy transport distance, and therefore within the zone itself[2]. The transport price is an independent variable as well. Rice stocks can be easily stored (compared to meat, refrigerated vegetables and fish) and transported, even by air. There is research

---

1. Tyers, Rodney, "Food Security in ASEAN: Potential Impacts of a Pacific Community", paper prepared for the conference held in Bangkok, June 3-5, 1982 on "ASEAN and Pacific Community".

2. UNESCAP, "Food Supply and Distribution in Asia and the Pacific", E/ESCAP/246, February 1982, p.348.

underway in Japan and the Philippines on developing new food
resources from sea-bed cultivation, but this would entail a
modification of cultural patterns of food consumption.

Serious efforts are still needed within the region to
assure sufficient nutritional levels for all parts of the
population:

Percentage of Population suffering from Malnutrition
(taken in average calorie intake)

	1965	1973
Indonesia	94	66
Philippines	73	70
Thailand	54	49
Malaysia	56	34
Korea	53	25

Source: World Bank Working Paper 374, March 1980.

As it is nearly impossible to create new cultivatable
land in the region, and food aid in terms of concessional loans
for market purchase or transfers of stocks are short term
solutions, it has become more evident to some observers that
policy changes will have to be implemented by the developing
countries of the region to give incentives to produce higher
yields on the now available surfaces if food needs are to be
met within the region[1]. The yield for developing nations
is still far below that of the developed nations in the zone:
the yield of rice ranged in 1980 from 1,968 kg/ha in Thailand
to over 5,000 kg/ha in Japan.

1. Villegas, Bernardo, "Resource-based Development in the
   Pacific Basin", op.cit. p.7ff.

Yield of Rice, Paddy
Unit: kg/ha

	1969-1971	1978	1979	1980
United States	5,087	5,026	5,155	4,935
Japan	5,485	6,416	5,986	5,128
Korea	4,628	6,790	6,392	4,918
Indonesia	2,346	2,887	2,985	3,187
Malaysia	2,396	2,596	2,761	2,698
Philippines	1,655	2,075	2,142	2,154
Thailand	1,947	2,115	1,822	1,968

Source: FAO Production Yearbook, 1980, Vol.34

        The introduction of more productive species of plant,
the expansion of the use of pesticides and fertilisers, as well
as improved irrigation methods (more rational use of smaller
farming surfaces) will require higher levels of investment in
the developing countries of the region[1].   This investment
may be stimulated by a regional focus of development, in which
the interest of the developing nations are matched by interests
from the industrial nations (stability of markets and hence
growth potential, new markets, trade agreements, transport
infrastructure).

        To contribute to the growth of production, to anticipate
sharp increases in food needs better and to manage food trade
on a more rational basis throughout the region have been
reasons put forward for the creation of an information centre
on food needs in the region[2].   Four principal tasks have
been suggested for such a centre:

   i.   contribute to the diffusion of appropriate technology
         in the agricultural sector;

1. The Pacific Basin Cooperation Study Group, Report on the
   Pacific Basin Cooperation Concept, Tokyo, May 1980.

2. UNESCAP, op.cit., Chapter III.

ii.   dissemination of relevant information concerning
       production, trade, management of stocks, price
       structures and the transport of agricultural products;

iii.   propose more rational management of agricultural
       imports, to limit the transport costs (see table
       below), and to form a common front when dealing with
       exporting nations;

iv.   to favour contractual arrangements in the long term
       that would strengthen links between nations of the
       region, stabilise price structures, provide markets
       and set up links between importing and exporting
       nations.

Cost of sea freight

Destination	Average rate en US$ per ton
Developing countries	24,91
Japan	12,36
Central Europe	9,73
Remainder of the world	15,36

Source: Journal of Agricultural Economics, February 1981, as quoted
          in the ESCAP report: "Food Supply and Distribution in Asia
          and the Pacific", February 1982.

        Such a system is now operative for the ASEAN nations of
the region. The FAO has also proposed studies that would
develop a series of "objective indicators" which would target
world food needs. Critics find that the ASEAN structure is too
localised and does not take into account links with non-ASEAN
nations, and the that FAO project with global ambitions, is too
large a proposed framework.

        Food stocks are a means of ensuring regional security in
the case of crisis. Although world-wide stocks
are currently sufficient for emergency situations, these are
not located in the Asia-Pacific side of the region, and they
would take time to transport across great distances. For the
most part, these emergency stocks are also wheat supplies. The
regional staple stock is rice, of which few substantial stocks
exist.

Since 1979, the ASEAN countries have constituted emergency stocks of rice, but the supply is low compared to potential needs (only 50,000 tons are currently stocked). This stock could be increased, and the locations diversified within the ASEAN itself. This set of stocks could be expanded to countries outside ASEAN, and to products other than rice, in order to stabilize the supply and the price of crucial food products. This regional feature could be a good complement to the proposed ASEBEX.

Commercial Aspects

The majority of the nations in the Asia-Pacific region have important agricultural-related trade. For this reason, price fluctuation and trade barrier tariffs pose problems at the regional level (given the high trading patterns within the region). Price instability in the past has led to important balance of payments problems, thus inducing problems at the level of national planning. A more systematic planning of stocks with larger capacities and easier transport access would lead to more manoeuvrability in times of crisis.

Certain industrial nations of the region have moved to restrict the import of agricultural products judged dispensible for reasons related to domestic policy. A larger regional concertation at the international level would harmonise these policies with suppliers and benefit, according to some advocates, all the nations of the region[1].

Liberalising trading restrictions on agricultural products (and most notably tropical products) has been the object of recent global negotiations[2]. Such negotiations within a regional association of nations with similar growth aims and policy orientations might be carried out with greater efficiency and speed[3].

The centrally-planned economies of the region have not been the objet of close study when discussing patterns of integration in the area. This arises from the apparent lack of interest on the part of the respective governments.

---

1. UNESCAP, op.cit., p.88ff.

2. UNCTAD V, Manila; Lomé II.

3. Joint Economic Committee, Pacific Region Interdependencies, Washington DC, June 1981, p.43.

ANNEX 1

PACIFIC BASIN DATA

	Area in thousand km^2	Population millions, 1981	GNP, 1980 billion US$	GNP/capita US$, 1980	Inflation per cent CPI, 1980
Australia	7,682	14.6	140.1	9,580	10.2
Canada	9,976	23.7	255	10,772	10.1
Japan	377	117.8	1,397	8,887	8.0
New Zealand	269	3.1	21.4	6,899	17.2
United States	9,356	230	2,576	11,319	13.5
South Korea	98	39.8	59.3	1,553	28.7
Hong Kong	1.1	5.1	13.6	2,720	15.9
Indonesia	1,904	149.4	66.8	439	21.0
Malaysia	329	14.3	23.7	1,763	6.7
Philippines	297	48.9	35.4	732	17.8
Papua New Guinea	289	3.3	1.9[*]	575[*]	17.5
Taiwan	36	18.2	32.3	2,720	15.9
Thailand	513	48.6	32.9	708	19.7
Singapore	0.6	2.4	6.4	2,650	8.5
Chili	756	10.9	20.5	1,886	35.1
Mexico	1,972	69.4	108	1,560	26.4
Peru	1,285	17.3	14.2	820	59.2
PRC	9,596	965	515	520	10.0[(e)]
USSR	22,402	264	1,300	4,925	1.3[*]
Vietnam	329	51	10.4	204	n.a.

* : figure for 1979
(e): estimated

Source: Asia Yearbook 1982, Far Eastern Economic Review

	Average Growth of Real GNP, 63/79	Average Growth of Real GNP, 75/79	Average Growth of Fixed Capital Formation, 63/79	Average Growth of Fixed Capital Formation, 75/79
Australia	4.6	2.5	2.6	0.5
Canada	4.8	3.6	4.8	1.3
Japan	7.3	5.2	9.0	6.2
New Zealand	n.a.	70/79: 2.5[1]	n.a.	n.a.
United States	3.3	4.6	2.1	1.4
South Korea	10.0	10.6	17.2	24.2
Hong Kong	8.9	11.6	7.5	19.2
Indonesia	6.1	7.0	69/79: 15.9	75/79: 11.3
Malaysia	70/77: 9.2	75/77: 9.6	71/77: 9.4	75/77: 9.0
Philippines	5.7	6.1	7.6	6.3
Papua New Guinea	65/76: 6.3	n.a.	65/76: - 2.3	n.a.
Taiwan	70/79: 8.2[1]	n.a.	n.a.	n.a.
Thailand	7.5	8.1	9.0	14.3
Singapore	8.5	8.3	11.0	6.6
Chili	63/78: 2.4	75/78: 6.4	63/78: - 0.4	75/78: 2.0
Mexico	6.0	5.2	7.5	4.7
Peru	3.7	0.9	2.8	- 11.5

Source: 1980 Yearbook of National Statistics, UN
except (1): Asia Society, Williamsburg Conference, 1980

	Public expenditure as % of GNP, 1980	Trade as % of GNP, 1980	Commercial Balance 1980, billion US$	Terms of Trade (1975 = 100)		
				1978	1980	1981
Australia	29	32	+ 2.9	83.9	87.5	86.6
Canada	22[1]	45[1]		n.a.	n.a.	n.a.
Japan	12	21	- 10.7	113.3	76.5	78.5
New Zealand	34	53	- 0.02	100	105	97
United States	21	18	- 25.4	95.5*	94.4	85.8
South Korea	19	67	- 4.2	128	103.9	101.6
Hong Kong	15	184	- 7.3	98.5*	97.2	94.9
Indonesia	20	49	+ 3.2	105	153	158
Malaysia	29	100	+ 2.0	141	140	114
Philippines	17	39	- 1.8	78.2**	65.9	n.a.
Papua New Guinea	n.a.	n.a.	+ 0.1	89.5	86.4	n.a.
Taiwan	11	98	+ 0.1	93.2#	81.9	78.6
Thailand	16	47	- 2.4	87.8	84.2	75.2
Singapore	18.5	189[1]	- 4.5	104.8**	101.2	n.a.

* : figures for 1977, 1979, 1981
**: 1972 = 100
: 1976 = 100

Source: Asia Yearbook 1983
except (1): Asia Society, Williamsburg Conference, 1980

	Trade within the region, except US and Japan, as % of Total Trade*	Trade with Japan, as % of Total Trade	Trade with the US, as % of Total Trade	Trade within the region, including US & Japan as % of Total Trade*
Australia	20[1]	21[1]	15[1]	56[1]
Canada	10[1]	5[1]	52[1]	67[1]
Japan	28[1]	-	19[1]	47[1]
New Zealand	41[1]	13[1]	12[1]	56[1]
United States	28[1]	11[1]	-	39[1]
South Korea	10	22	24	56
Hong Kong	24	14	19	57
Indonesia	16	43	17	76
Malaysia	28	23	16	67
Philippines	14	23	25	62
Papua New Guinea	n.a.	n.a.	n.a.	n.a.
Taiwan	14	19	29	62
Thailand	14	19	10	47
Singapore	40	13.2	13.5	67

Source: Asia Yearbook 1982
         except (1): compiled from the trade matrix given in Annex 1, p.57.

* Columns 1 and 4 do not include figures for Latin America

	Balance of Payments: million SDRs 1981[1]	Net Capital Flow: million US$, 1979[2]	Debt Service as % of Exports of Goods and Services, 1980[3]
Australia	- 170	+ 17.2	
Canada	- 410	n.a.	
Japan	- 4,869	+ 1,804	
New Zealand	- 87	+ 649	
United States	- 3,941	-17,400	
South Korea	- 233	+ 800	12.2
Hong Kong	n.a.	n.a.	n.a.
Indonesia	1980: - 1,144	+ 1,804	8.0
Malaysia	113	n.a.	2.3
Philippines	- 271	+ 390	7.0
Papua New Guinea	- 19	+ 95.4	6.0
Taiwan	n.a.	+ 1,206	5.1
Thailand	- 73	+ 780	n.a.
Singapore	- 1,337	+ 1,458	1.1

Sources: (1) International Financial Statistics, Feb. 1983
(2) Asia Yearbook 1982
(3) World Bank Report 1982

Trade Matrix 1980   (Exports)

	Advanced Countries	Australia	Canada	Japan	New Zealand	United States	Asian NICs	ASEAN Countries	Islands Countries	Latin America	PEC Area	World Total
Advanced Countries	66,998	8,772	38,431	31,092	2,414	76,289	29,439	25,149	1,145	28,776	241,507	446,698
Australia	9,963		470	5,871	1,043	2,549	1,270	1,766	696	101	13,796	22,601
Canada	45,488	576		3,751	96	41,065	744	795	5	1,070	48,102	67,527
Japan	38,443	3,409	2,449		744	31,905	15,736	13,075	252	4,573	72,079	130,460
New Zealand	2,231	714	117	680		720	206	366	150	72	3,025	5,407
United States	60,873	4,093	35,395	20,790	595		11,274	9,177	42	22,930	105,296	220,703
Asian NICs	28,042	1,137	1,219	9,074	145	16,467	3,652	5,081	48	1,051	37,874	60,021
ASEAN Countries	31,948	1,541	303	18,061	519	11,424	5,160	11,401	204	399	49,112	67,063
Island Countries	739	138	24	430	51	96	14	54	18	6	831	1,523
Latin America	18,347	22	570	2,072	9	15,674	389	38	0	2,911	21,685	34,454
PEC Area	236,074	11,610	40,547	62,729	3,138	120,050	38,654	41,723	1,415	33,143	351,009	609,659
World Total	484,496	22,179	62,566	141,284	5,472	252,995	65,434	64,796	1,920	39,481	656,127	*1,886,000 *1,936,000

Unit : million US dollars
Source: Pacific Economic Community Statistics, PBEC/Japan National Committee, Tokyo, 1982
 * above : Exports
  below : Imports

American Direct Investment in the Pacific Basin Area

	1970 Amount	1970 %	1975 Amount	1975 %	1976 Amount	1976 %	1977 Amount	1977 %	1978 Amount	1978 %	1979 Amount	1979 %	1980 Amount	1980 %
Australia	3,304	11.0	5,065	11.2	5,460	11.1	5,739	11.2	6,368	11.5	7,165	11.7	7,584	11.3
Canada	22,790	76.2	31,038	68.7	33,927	69.1	35,200	68.5	37,280	67.3	40,243	65.9	44,640	66.7
Japan	1,483	4.9	3,339	7.4	3,787	7.7	4,143	8.1	4,963	8.9	6,208	10.2	6,274	9.4
New Zealand	184	0.6	365	0.8	404	0.8	421	0.8	466	0.8	524	0.8	579	0.9
United States	-	-	-	-	-	-	-	-	-	-	-	-	-	-
Hong Kong	-	-	-	-	-	-	-	-	-	-	1,770	2.8	1,969	2.9
Korea	-	-	-	-	-	-	-	-	-	-	689	1.1	587	0.8
Taiwan	-	-	-	-	-	-	-	-	-	-	393	0.6	510	0.8
Indonesia	-	-	1,587	3.5	1,475	3.0	1,122	2.1	1,245	2.2	1,191	1.9	1,334	1.9
Malaysia	-	-	-	-	-	-	-	-	-	-	561	0.9	618	0.9
Philippines	701	2.3	738	1.6	831	1.7	913	1.8	1,003	1.8	1,254	2.0	1,244	1.8
Singapore	-	-	-	-	-	-	-	-	-	-	860	1.4	1,196	1.8
Thailand	-	-	-	-	-	-	-	-	-	-	200	0.3	360	0.5
Other Western Pacific	1,450	4.8	3,055	6.7	3,253	6.6	3,845	7.5	4,076	7.3	-	-	-	-
Total	29,912	100	45,187	100	49,086	100	51,383	100	55,401	100	61,058	100	66,895	100
Total as % of worldwide American Investment	38.2%		36.4%		35.7%		34.2%		32.9%		32.6%		31.3%	

Unit: million US$
Source: US Department of Commerce

Japanese Direct Investments in the Pacific Basin Area

	1976		1977		1978		1979		1980		1951-1980	
	Amount	%	Amount	%	Amount	%	Amount	%	Amount	%	Amount	%
Australia	137	6.4	146	8.3	204	6.9	566	19	431	13.4	2,165	9.8
Canada	86	4.0	48	2.7	82	2.8	93	3.1	112	3.5	920	4.2
Japan	-	-	-	-	-	-	-	-	-	-	-	-
New Zealand	5	0.2	5	0.3	2	0.06	1	0.03	8	0.2	126	0.6
United States	663	30.8	686	39	1,283	43.6	1,345	45.2	1,484	46.2	8,878	40.4
Hong Kong	69	3.2	109	6.2	159	5.4	225	7.5	156	4.9	1,095	5.0
Korea	102	4.7	95	5.4	222	7.5	95	3.2	35	1.1	1,137	5.2
Taiwan	28	1.3	18	1.0	40	1.4	39	1.3	47	1.5	370	1.7
Indonesia	929	43.1	425	24.2	610	20.7	150	5.0	529	16.5	4,424	20.2
Malaysia	54	2.5	69	3.9	48	1.6	33	1.1	146	4.5	650	3.0
Philippines	15	0.7	27	1.5	53	1.8	102	3.4	78	2.4	615	2.8
Singapore	27	1.3	66	3.8	174	5.9	255	8.6	140	4.4	936	4.3
Thailand	19	0.9	49	2.8	32	1.1	55	1.8	33	1.0	396	1.8
Island Countries	20	0.9	14	0.7	33	1.1	14	0.4	10	0.3	235	1.0
Total	2,154	100	1,757	100	2,942	100	2,973	100	3,209	100	21,947	100
Total as % of world-wide Japanese investments	62.2%		62.6%		63.9%		59.5%		68.3%		60.1%	

Unit: million US$
Source: MITI

ASEAN Pattern of Trade: Shares of Exports and Imports by Regions
(Selected periods, per cent)

	Intra-ASEAN		Intra-Pacific		EEC		Rest of the world		World	
	Exports	Imports	Exports	Imports	Exports	Imports	Exports	Imports	Exports	Imports
Indonesia										
1965-1967	7.9	5.8	58.6	63.8	25.4	24.4	16.0	11.7	100	100
1971-1973	12.2	8.8	84.3	72.3	12.1	20.3	3.6	7.5	100	100
1977-1979	12.7	11.8	85.1	68.6	7.8	17.8	7.1	13.5	100	100
Malaysia										
1965-1967	26.7	18.4	67.1	54.0	17.3	26.1	15.7	19.9	100	100
1971-1973	24.9	14.9	65.6	62.5	20.2	21.7	14.2	15.8	100	100
1977-1979	18.9	14.6	68.9	69.2	18.5	17.8	12.6	13.1	100	100
Philippines										
1965-1967	0.8	5.5	80.4	74.2	14.0	14.2	5.6	11.6	100	100
1971-1973	1.9	4.3	83.8	73.3	12.6	14.6	3.6	12.1	100	100
1977-1979	4.7	5.9	73.3	66.2	19.2	13.0	7.6	20.9	100	100
Singapore										
1965-1967	39.8	33.9	60.4	67.5	12.6	16.4	26.9	16.2	100	100
1971-1973	27.2	25.1	66.1	73.2	15.3	14.9	18.6	12.0	100	100
1977-1979	23.4	27.4	66.2	70.1	12.9	11.3	20.9	18.5	100	100
Thailand										
1965-1967	22.3	3.9	60.6	58.6	16.3	20.7	23.0	20.7	100	100
1971-1973	18.7	3.2	67.2	64.6	16.6	19.6	16.2	15.9	100	100
1977-1979	17.2	6.0	59.3	61.2	23.7	14.4	16.9	24.4	100	100

Source: ESCAP Secretariat; unnumbered working paper prepared for the Conference held in Bangkok, June 3-5, 1982: "ASEAN and Pacific Cooperation".

Compound Annual Growth Rate of ASEAN Total Merchandise Exports
(Percentage)

	Indonesia		Malaysia		Philippines		Singapore		Thailand	
	1965-72	1972-77	1965-72	1972-77	1965-72	1972-77	1965-72	1972-77	1965-72	1972-77
To: All destinations	12.7	31.4	5.7	25.6	5.1	17.6	12.7	25.6	6.7	22.8
Total Pacific	19.7	31.7	5.9	26.7	6.1	14.8	13.8	25.4	8.8	19.9
ASEAN	30.9	36.7	4.8	19.5	24.6	43.1	6.1	22.9	1.2	20.1
Indonesia	-	-	102.0	6.6	13.7	39.7	136.0	27.6	4.1	23.8
Malaysia	68.8	- 3.9	-	-	57.2	67.4	2.3	18.7	- 8.0	20.6
Philippines	- 5.0	106.9	4.6	25.3	-	-	16.0	41.8	3.2	- 7.8
Singapore	52.7	37.9	4.2	18.5	25.0	37.7	-	-	9.5	20.3
Thailand	- 48.9	88.8	6.9	42.0	45.0	32.5	14.8	32.3	-	-
Australia	- 19.3	43.9	- 1.1	23.5	10.6	39.4	25.2	18.8	22.6	30.4
Canada	4.2	56.6	- 0.6	9.4	19.3	32.9	18.8	22.6	30.4	36.0
China	0.0	0.0	47.3	21.9	38.9	68.6	2.7	19.2	38.9	90.9
Hong Hong	- 6.4	27.2	20.1	17.1	30.9	31.3	18.9	29.7	8.3	14.7
Japan	29.5	26.7	5.6	32.6	9.0	9.9	24.9	31.7	9.5	19.7
Korea, Republic of	68.1	39.9	38.2	18.9	8.1	29.8	50.9	42.5	56.3	26.2
New Zealand	- 5.3	61.8	- 0.2	35.8	55.1	17.7	2.6	33.8	50.9	23.0
Other Asia-Pacific	99.0	35.9	15.5	38.2	6.2	5.7	30.0	31.9	33.4	3.9
United States	8.6	39.2	4.3	33.7	2.9	13.6	35.3	24.2	17.5	23.5
EEC	1.2	25.3	7.7	22.5	1.3	26.5	15.1	22.6	6.5	32.8
Rest of the World	- 11.3	39.4	1.7	26.1	- 1.6	33.0	8.3	28.7	0.8	22.6

Source: ESCAP Secretariat

ASEAN Countries' Exports and Imports by Broad Commodity Groups, 1979
(million US$)

	Indonesia		Malaysia		Philippines		Singapore		Thailand	
	Exports	Imports	Exports	Imports	Exports	Imports	Exports	Imports	Exports	Imports
Food and live animals	1,208	1,308	495	938	852	412	870	1,174	2,454	210
Beverages and tobacco	58	21	10	85	35	52	61	95	62	60
Crude materials (excel. fuels)	3,064	367	4,128	389	1,236	306	2,030	1,430	874	548
Mineral fuels	10,166	798	2,021	950	11	1,469	3,411	4,451	2	1,610
Animal, vegetable oil, fat	222	31	1,380	14	748	20	395	382	1	27
Chemicals	64	1,012	60	799	112	732	517	1,002	36	1,057
Basic manufactures	1,571	1,385	1,520	1,335	419	1,012	1,307	2,640	1,123	1,269
Machines, transport, equipment	116	2,277	1,160	2,915	81	1,798	3,780	5,219	195	1,841
Misc. manufactured goods	81	227	276	362	471	150	976	1,010	329	200
Goods not classified by kind	40	46	34	62	608	663	26	235	131	348

Source: ESCAP Secretariat; unnumbered working paper prepared for the Conference held in Bangkok, June 3-5, 1982: "ASEAN and Pacific Cooperation".

Reserves in Primary Energy Resources

	Oil (a)(b)	Natural gas (a)(b)(c)	Coal (d)(e)	Hydro-Electricity (f)
Australia	2,130	5,270	27,353	n.a.
Canada	6,800	14,380	9,381	n.a.
Japan	55	100	1,006	n.a.
New Zealand	110	1,020	144	n.a.
USA	26,500	37,380	177,588	n.a.
China (PRC)	20,000	4,490	98,883	n.a.
Indonesia	9,600	3,858	1,430	30,000
Korea, R.	-	-	386	5,514
Malaysia	2,800	4,200	-	1,319
Philippines	25	-	-	7,504
Thailand	-	1,360	-	6,242
Regional total	77,620	72,508	316,171	n.a.
% World total	(640,569) 12.1%	(460,042) 15.7%	(636,364) 49%	n.a.

(a) unit: million barrels of oil equivalent
(b) proven reserves
(c) associated and non-associated gas
(d) unit: million tons of coal equivalent
(e) technically and economically recoverable reserves
(f) estimated gross theoretical capacity, in megawatts

Country	CEREALS			MEAT		
	Imports	Exports	Balance	Imports	Exports	Balance
Australia	491	1,946,677	1,946,186	1,559	833,799	832,230
Canada	138,325	2,157,178	2,018,853	95,002	242,711	147,709
Japan	2,447,310	82,646	- 2,364,664	523,375	4,239	- 519,136
New Zealand	6,272	11,359	5,087	2,656	644,387	641,731
United States	19,254	11,290,580	11,271,326	758,890	730,761	- 28,129
Sub-total	2,611,652	15,488,430	12,876,778	1,381,482	2,455,897	1,074,415
Hong Kong	81,176	1,732	- 79,444	139,220	1,727	- 137,493
Indonesia	355,077	2,539	- 352,468	1,298	1,600	+ 302
Korea (South)	514,287	19	- 514,268	15,612	9,238	- 6,374
Malaysia	133,035	1,050	- 131,985	20,400	-	- 20,400
Philippines	105,247	20,377	- 84,870	6,961	350	- 6,611
Thailand	20,932	61,813	+ 40,881	392	18,965	+ 18,573
Sub-total	1,209,684	87,530	- 1,122,154	183,883	31,880	- 152,003
Grand total	3,821,336	15,575,960	11,754,624	1,565,365	2,487,777	922,412

Unit: Cereals, 10,000 metric tons
      Meat, 1,000 metric tons
Source: FAO Trade Yearbook, 1980

Aid Flows to Asia/Pacific Developing Countries:
ODA Net Receipts in 1981

	Total ODA (1)	Total Bilateral ODA From DAC Countries (2)	Part of OECD Countries of the region in (2)* (in percent)
ASEAN	1922.3	1582.1	69%
Indonesia	975.4	799.5	59%
Malaysia	142.0	117.3	65%
Philippines	376.5	331.0	84%
Singapore	21.8	18.4	68%
Thailand	406.6	315.9	79%
EAST ASIAN NICS	347.9	323.7	93%
Hong Kong	9.5	3.6	56%
Korea (South)	330.6	325.9	95%
Taiwan	7.8	- 5.8	-
OTHER PACIFIC	977.7	774.4	61%
Papua New Guinea	335.9	274.7	98%
Pacific Islands	641.8	499.7	41%
TOTAL ASIA/PACIFIC	3247.9	2680.2	70%

* Australia, Canada, Japan, New Zealand, USA

Unit: million US$

Source: Geographical Distribution of Financial Flows in Developing Countries, OECD, Paris, 1982

ANNEX 2

- SYNOPTIC TABLE OF EXISTING ORGANISATIONS
- DESCRIPTION OF SOME EXISTING ORGANISATIONS
- LIST OF PACIFIC COOPERATION-RELATED ACTIVITIES (1968-1983)
- REPORT OF THE BANGKOK CONFERENCE (JUNE 1982)

SUMMARY OF EXISTING ORGANISATIONS

Nature / Date of creation	NON REGIONAL FOCUS					REGIONAL FOCUS									
COUNTRY	IBRD 1945	IMF 1945	GATT 1948	OECD 1961	UNCTAD 1964	ESCAP 1947	SPC 1947	COLOMBO 1950	ANZUS 1952	ADB 1965	NAFTA 1966	ASEAN 1967	PBEC 1967	PAFTAD 1968	SPEC 1972
Australia	x	x	x	x	-	x	x	x	x	x	x	-	x	x	x
Canada	x	x	x	x	x	-	-	x	-	x	-	-	x	x	-
Japan	x	x	x	x	x	x	-	x	-	x	-	-	x	x	-
New Zealand	x	x	x	x	x	x	x	x	x	x	x	-	x	x	x
United States	x	x	x	x	x	x	x	x	x	x	x	-	x	x	-
Hong-Kong	x	x	-	-	x	x (2)	-	x	-	x	-	-	-	x	-
Indonesia	x	x	x	-	x	x	-	x	-	x	-	x	-	x	-
Korea (Rep. of)	x	x	x (1)	-	x	x	-	x	-	x	-	-	-	x	-
Malaysia	x	x	x	-	-	x	x	x	-	x	-	x	-	x	-
Papua New Guinea	x	x	x	-	x	x	x	x	-	x	-	-	-	x	x
Philippines	x	x	x	-	x	x	-	x	-	x	-	x	-	x	-
Singapore	x	x	x	-	x	x	-	x	-	x	-	x	-	x	-
Taiwan	-	-	-	-	-	x	x	x	-	x	-	-	-	x	-
Thailand	x	x	x	-	x	x	-	x	-	x	-	x	-	x	-
Other Pacific (Oceania, etc...)	x	x	x	-	x	x	x	x	-	x	-	-	-	x	x
Other Outside Pacific	x	x	x	x	x	x	x	x	-	x	-	-	-	-	-
Concerned with:															
1. Trade (general)															
a. Tariffs	x	-	x	x	x	-	-	-	-	x	-	x	-	x	x
b. Other trade barriers	-	-	x	-	x	-	-	-	-	-	-	-	x	x	x
c. Foreign exchange problem	-	x	x	-	x	-	-	-	-	x	-	-	-	x	-
2. Investment or Aid	x	-	-	x	x	-	x	-	-	x	-	-	-	x	-
3. Harmonisation or discussion of economic policies	-	x	x	x	x	-	-	x	-	-	-	x	x	x	x
4. Common front to outside	-	-	-	-	x	-	-	-	-	-	-	x	-	-	-
5. Research and discussion	-	-	-	-	-	-	-	-	-	-	-	x	-	-	-
6. Military security	x	-	-	x	-	x	x	x	x	x	-	x	-	x	x

Notes: (1) de facto member, pending final decision
(2) associate member

Description of Some Existing Organisations in the Region[1]

ESCAP
(Economic and Social Commission for Asia and the Pacific
of the United Nations)

Membership (1976)

Afghanistan	Japan	Singapore
Australia	Kampuchea	Soc. Rep. of Vietnam
Bangladesh	Kiribati	Solomon Islands
Bhutan	Korea	Sri Lanka
Brunei	Laos	Thailand
Burma	Malaysia	The Pacific Islands
China, Peoples Rep.	Maldives	Tonga
Cook Islands(2)	Mongolia	Tuvalu(2)
Democratic Kampuchea	Nauru	UK
Fiji	Nepal	USA
France	Netherlands	USSR
Guam	New Zealand	Vanuake(2)
Hong Kong(2)	Niue(2)	Western Samoa
India	Pakistan	
Indonesia	Papua New Guinea	
Iran	Philippines	

Purpose

The Commission was established to initiate and participate in measures for facilitating economic and social development in Asia and the Pacific and for strengthening relations among those nations, and between them and the rest of the world.

Background

Formerly this Commission was titled ECAFE (Economic Commission for Asia and the Far East), which was established in 1947. In its deliberations, the Commission covers a wide range of issues and projects. ECAFE was virtually the only semi-regional organisation (along with the Colombo Plan) until the 1960s. ESCAP has established a number of subsidiary bodies, including the Asian and Pacific Development Centre, Asian Highway Coordinating Committee, Asian Statistical Institute, the Committee for Coordination of Joint Prospecting for Mineral Resources in the Asian Offshore Areas, and the Typhoon Committee.

---

1. Selected and adapted from An Asian-Pacific Regional Economic Organisation: An Exploratory Concept Paper, US Government Printing Office, Washington, 1979, p.66ff., corrected by the OECD Development Centre.

2. Associate Members

SPC
(South Pacific Commission)

Membership (as of 1981)

Participating governments:

Australia	New Zealand	United Kingdom
Cook Islands	Niue	United States
Fiji Papua New Guinea	Western Samoa	
France	Solomon Islands	
Nauru	Tuvalu	

Countries and territories also entitled to be represented:

American Samoa	New Caledonia	Tokelau
French Polynesia	Norfolk Island	Tonga
Guam Northern Mariane	Vanuatu	
Kiribati	Islands	Wallis and Futuna
Marshall Islands	Palau	Islands

Purpose

Each territory has its own programme of development activities. Created in 1947, the Commission assists these programmes by bringing people together for discussion and study, by research into some of the problems common to the region, by providing expert advice and assistance and by disseminating technical information.

Background

The Conference is held annually and since 1974 has combined the former South Pacific Conference, attended by delegates from the countries and territories within the Commission's area of action, and the former Commission Session, attended by representatives of the participating governments. Each government and territorial administration has the right to send a representative and alternates to the Conference and each representative (or in his absence an alternate) has the right to cast one vote on behalf of the government or territorial administration which he represents.

The Conference examines and adopts the Commission's work programme and budget for the coming year, and discusses any other matters within the competence of the Commission.

COLOMBO PLAN

Membership (as of 1981)

Afghanistan	Iran	Pakistan
Australia	Japan	Papua New Guinea
Bangladesh	Korea	Philippines
Bhutan	Laos	Singapore
Burma	Malaysia	Sri Lanka
Cambodia	Maldives	Thailand
Canada	Nepal	United Kingdom
India	New Zealand	United States
Indonesia		

Purpose

The Colombo Plan was organised to channel development aid into Asia - from developed donor members to LDC members.

Background

The Plan began in 1950. Its structure remains informal, with only a small permanent administrative group. Periodic meetings of members review past aid projects and suggests future areas for aid. Donor nations pick a number of their development aid projects they desire to attach to the Colombo Plan. It also operates a school (since 1975) called the Colombo Plan Staff College for Technical Education (in Singapore).

ANZUS PACT
(Australia, New Zealand, United States Pact)

Membership

Australia	New Zealand	United States

Purpose

Basically ANZUS is a mutual security pact, providing for joint action in case of military attack and for peacetime military consultation and cooperation.

Background

ANZUS began in 1952. The foreign ministers meet once a year with additional meetings of military representatives as needed; more recent discussions have focused attention on the non-military aspects of security.

ADB
(Asian Development Bank)

Membership (as of 1971)

Afghanistan	India	Pakistan
Australia	Indonesia	Philippines
Bangladesh	Italy	Singapore
Belgium	Japan	Solomon Islands
Burma	Kampuchea	Sri Lanka
Canada	Kiribati	Sweden
Ceylon	Kampuchea	Switzerland
Cook Islands	Korea	Papua New Guinea
Denmark	Laos	Taiwan
Fiji	Malaysia	Thailand
Finland	Maldives	Tongo
France	Nepal	United Kingdom
Fed. Rep. of Germany	Netherlands	United States
Hong Kong	New Zealand	Vietnam
	Norway	Western Samoa

Purpose

The bank's purpose is to promote and finance investment in the ESCAP region for development purposes.

Background

ADB is a regional development bank to loan funds provided by the developed industrial nations members to Asian LDC members. Organised in 1965, membership is open to all ESCAP members (and non-ESCAP developed nations). Interest rates are flexible and set separately for each loan. It coordinates its lending program to some degree with World Bank lending activities in the region. Operation is overseen by a board of governors with voting strength proportional to the capital contribution to the bank. Japan and the United States are the major capital contributors. The president customarily is a Japanese.

NAFTA
(New Zealand-Australia Free Trade Area)

Membership

New Zealand   Australia

Membership is potentially open to new entrants.

Purpose

Its main purposes are to provide for limited free trade between the two countries within the framework of GATT and for regular bilateral consultation on trade and economic policy matters.

Background

NAFTA was founded in 1966. The regular provisions of the free trade agreement do not cover all bilateral trade, but the possibility of trade sharing arrangements has been explicitly allowed.

ASEAN
(Association of South-East Asian Nations)

Membership

Indonesia   Philippines   Thailand
Malaysia   Singapore

Purpose

ASEAN's goals are the acceleration of economic growth and cultural progress among its members, cooperation on agriculture and industry, expansion of trade, and development of a common negotiating front towards major trading nations.

Background

ASEAN was established in 1967 at Bangkok, from ASA (Association of Southeast Asia) which consisted of Malaya, the Philippines and Thailand. ASEAN has established regular contacts with the GATT, the EEC, Japan, Australia, New Zealand and Canada. The Declaration of Concord signed in 1976 includes the pursuit of political stability in the region. In the fields of trade and industry the countries of ASEAN have concluded a Preferential Trade Arrangement and agreed to set up joint industrial projects in areas of common interest. ASEAN operates with annual meetings at ministerial level. There are also periodic meetings of representatives from member nations, plus permanent (standing) groups on specific topics under the standing committees.

PBEC
(Pacific Basin Economic Council)

Membership

Members consist of major business firms in the following countries:

Australia	Japan	United States
Canada	New Zealand	

Purpose

PBEC exists to strengthen economic and business relations among its members, and to promote economic and social progress in the Pacific Area.

Background

PBEC was organised in 1967, holding its first meeting in 1968. It now has 400 member companies within the 5 member countries. A private group, PBEC holds annual meetings; there is no permanent central organisation other than small secretariats.

PAFTAD
(Pacific Trade and Development Conferences)

Membership

PAFTAD is guided by a steering committee of members from Australia, Japan, Canada, Southeast Asia, and the United States. Participants from other Pacific countries have been involved in its meetings.

Purpose

PAFTAD promotes policy-oriented academic study and discussion of Pacific Area economic issues. It serves as the major intellectual resource for those in the Pacific area interested in the analysis of regional economic prospects.

Background

This is an informal private academic conference series originally begun in 1968 with Japanese Foreign Ministry support to consider a proposal for a Pacific Free Trade Area. Ten conferences have been held since that time in different Pacific countries, involving a wide group of policy-interested economists, to discuss regional foreign economic policy issues mainly among the Pacific Five and Western Pacific developing economies. Some conferences have, however, included Latin American and Soviet participation.

SPEC
(The South Pacific Bureau for Economic Cooperation)

Membership (as of 1981)

Australia	Nauru	Solomon Islands
Cook Islands	New Zealand	Tonga
Fiji	Nive	Tuvalu
Kiribati	Papua New Guinea	Vanciatu
		Western Samoa

Purpose

The Bureau facilitates cooperation and consultatioin between its members on trade, economic development, transportation, tourism and other related matters.

Background

Recommended by the South Pacific Forum meeting in September 1972, the Bureau was formally founded in 1973 and absorbed the Pacific Islands Producers' Association (PIPA). It has a secretariat and a committee formed of one member from each participating country. Australia and New Zealand each contribute one-third of the budget and the island countries the rest.

LIST OF SELECTED MAJOR PACIFIC COOPERATION-RELATED ACTIVITIES 1968-1983
Based on a list prepared by the JCIE for the Pacific Basin Economic Council, Japan National Committee,
dated March 31, 1981; updated by the OECD Development Centre, March 1983

TITLE	SPONSORING ORGANISATION	DATE/DURATION	CONTENT
1st PAFTAD Conference	Japan Economic Research Centre	January 1968	Interest in the PAFTAD concept was discussed.
2nd PAFTAD Conference	East-West Center, Hawaii	1969	Debate on Free Trade Zones
3rd PAFTAD Conference	Sydney, Australia	1970	Direct Foreign Investment in Asia and the Pacific.
4th PAFTAD Conference	Ottawa, Canada	October 1971	Obstacles to Trade in the Pacific Region.
5th PAFTAD Conference	Tokyo, Japan	January 1973	Structural Adjustment in Asia-Pacific Trade.
6th PAFTAD Conference	Mexico City	July 1974	Technology Transfer in Pacific Economic Development.
7th PAFTAD Conference	Auckland, New Zealand	August 1975	Cooperation and Development in the Asia-Pacific Region, Relations between Large and Small Countries.
8th PAFTAD Conference	Pattaya, Thailand	July 1976	Trade and Employment for Asian Developing Countries.
9th PAFTAD Conference	San Francisco, USA	August 1977	Mineral Resources in the Pacific Area.

Project/Title	Date	Institution	Description
Research on Pan-Pacific Community Concept (project)	March 1979-1980	Korea International Economic Institute (Korea)	Research on present status and future prospects of Pan-Pacific Community concept and its implications on ASEAN and Korea.
10th PAFTAD Conference	March 1979	Canberra, Australia	ASEAN in the changing Pacific and World Economy.
An Asian-Pacific Regional Economic Organisation: An Exploratory Concept Paper (report)	July 1979	Senate Committee on Foreign Relations (USA)	Evaluation of proposals for a Pacific area regional economic association. Emphasised US interest in a possible formation of an OPTAD.
The Pacific Community: Toward A Role for Latin America (conference)	October 18-23, 1979	Institute of International Studies, University of Chile (Chile)	Discussed the economic, political and cultural dimensions of the cooperation in the Pacific Basin and the actual and potential role of Latin America in the trans-Pacific cooperation.
Analysis of Economic Data on the Pacific Basin (research project)	1979	Brookings Institution (USA)	As a State Department Consultant for Pacific Affairs, Dr. Krause received a grant to analyse economic data on the Pacific Basin and the research is currently underway.
Asian Pacific Economic Community (research project)	October 1979-September 1981	Asiatic Research Center (ARC) Korea University (Korea)	A two-year project to examine the various proposals for economic integration in the Asia-Pacific region. A seminar was conducted on May 4-6, 1981 by a number of participants from the Canberra Conference to discuss papers prepared for the ARC project, focusing on political-economic and cultural affairs in the region.

Asia-Pacific in the 1980s: Toward Greater Symmetry in Economic Inter-dependence (conference)	Centre for Strategic and Inter-national Studies (Indonesia)	January 11-13, 1980	Discussed the possibility of creating some kind of an Asian-Pacific con-sultative body as well as the ever-increasing importance of the role of Pacific Basin countries.
Fourth Asian Dialogue-OISO Symposium	Japan Center for International Exchange (Japan)	January 19-21, 1980	Discussed the divergence and con-vergence of Perceptions on Pan-Pacific Cooperation, and attempted to elicit interest in and perspectives on the Pacific Community concept from the ASEAN countries.
Pacific Community Concept (seminar)	Rockefeller Foundation (USA)	March 31, 1980	To review recent evolution of the concept of a Pacific Community.
Pacific Basin Cooperation: What It Means for New Zealand (seminar)	New Zealand Institute of Inter-national Affairs (New Zealand)	March 31-April 1, 1980	This international seminar discussed the Pacific Community concept and the alternative approaches for New Zealand. Special consideration was given to the role of the small island countries in the South Pacific.
The Pacific Basin Cooperation Concept (report)	The Pacific Basin Cooperation Study Group (Japan)	May 1980	Conducted intensive study of Pacific Basin Cooperation commissioned by the late Prime Minister Ohira to explore the possibility of economic and cultural cooperation in the region and the establishment of some kind of private organisation to act as cooperation channel. The group was dissolved after the presentation of the Final Report which was discussed at the ANU Pacific Seminar in September 1980.

Business Cooperation Between Asia-Pacific and Japan in the 1980s (conference)	The Export-Import Bank of Japan	May 26-27, 1980	Discussed economic cooperation in the region such as investment activities, industrialisation, technology transfer, natural resource development, balance of payments, financialities between Asia-Pacific and Japan, etc.
Forum on the Pacific Basin Growth, Security and Community (conference)	The Asia and World Forum (Taipei)	May 28-30, 1980	To explore further the various perspectives on the Pacific Basin. Representatives of ten countries in the Pacific Basin participated.
Trans-Pacific Agricultural Trade (workshop)	East-West Resource System Institute, East-West Center (USA)	July 21-25, 1980	Discussed research on agricultural and food trade and interdependent relationships in the Pacific region. Research topics include fishing in the Pacific region, food trade policies and setting of prices, and analyses of world market for soybean, etc.
Pacific Community Seminar (conference)	The Australian National University (Australia)	September 15-18, 1980	Seminar was held after an agreement between the late Prime Minister Ohira and Prime Minister Fraser. The seminar invited participants from 11 Pacific countries and the South Pacific Islands. Agreement was reached on the formation of a Pacific Cooperation Committee on a non-governmental basis to examine a possible institutional structure.
11th PAFTAD Conference	Seoul, Korea	Sept. 1980	Role of the Advanced Developing Economies in the Region.

The 7th Asian Round Table (conference)	Asia Club (Japan)	October 10-11, 1980	Discussed new political trends in Asia under the overall theme of "In Search of a Creative Pattern of Interaction in Asia", including values, culture and interactions, prospects for Pan-Pacific cooperation, particularly its pros and cons, in view of geographical conditions, and gaps of economic levels in the region.
Coexistence of Differing Systems in the Pacific Region: Styles and Mechanisms for Crises Management	Williamsburg Meeting	November 13-16, 1980	Discussed, among other issues, the nature of interdependence among Pacific countries and examined steps to be taken to further the Pacific Community idea.
The Pacific Basin Project (research project)	Aspen Institute for Humanistic Studies/Program in International Affairs (USA), Hubert H. Humphrey Institute of Public Affairs, University of Minnesota	1980-1982	Workshop on five functional areas of regional cooperation identified as: (1) Changing Industrial Geography; (2) Management of the Pacific Marine Commons; (3) Pacific Energy Futures; (4) Pacific Communications: From Remoteness to Regional Community; and (5) Institutional Futures in the Pacific Basin.
Strengthening Pacific Area Economic Cooperation (seminar)	Pacific Forum (USA)	November 29- December 1, 1980	Two sessions were devoted to a wide-ranging discussion of the Pacific Community concept. Considerable attention was devoted to the relationship between ASEAN and the Pacific Community.
Canada and the Pacific, Agenda for the 80s (research project)	Joint Center on Modern East Asia, University of Toronto and York University	1981-1984	Three-year programme focussing on three subjects: (1) trade and economic development; (2) political and strategic considerations; (3) the socio-cultural context.

Congressional Study Group on the Emerging Pacific Community	Georgetown University, CSIS	1981-1982	3 senators and 2 congressmen co-chaired this programme. The study group met on Capitol Hill every four to six weeks. The project ended with a major academic conference in 1982.
Workshop on the Pacific Community (Seoul, Korea)	Asiatic Research Center of Korea University	May 4-6, 1981	Stress on political issues in the Pacific Basin and attention focussed on ASEAN countries.
Conference on "Factors Affecting Growth Prospects in the Pacific Basin" (Hong Kong)	PBEC	May 4-7, 1981	280 senior executives from fifteen Pacific Basin countries attended this PBEC International General Meeting.
Pacific Asian Executive Programme	Pacific Asian Management Institute, University of Hawaii	July 1981-August 1982	Programme designed for Pacific area business managers.
12th PAFTAD Conference on "Renewable Resources of the Pacific Area"	International Development Research Center (IDRC)	September 7-11, 1981	The key areas examined were fisheries, forests and energy.
Symposium on "Trade tensions in the Pacific, how can they be reduced" (Capitol Hill, Washington)	PPCA and Asia Society	September 23, 1981	Saburo Okita and William Brock, US Trade Representative were the featured speakers. This symposium gave special attention to regional and multilateral concerns about trade.
Programme on Pacific Community	San Francisco State University	September-December 1981	Lecture series to explore Pacific inter-dependencies and key issues involved in the formation of a Pacific Community.

Conference on "US Trade Policies, and the prospects for Pacific-US Trade and Investments" (Washington)	US-Asia Institute	October 2-3, 1981	Several leading US administration trade spokesmen addressed the conference.
Conference on "Emerging Trends in Trade, Finance, Technology, and Economic Growth - Conflict or Cooperation Ahead"	Pacific Forum (Hawaii)	November 13-15, 1981	Exchange of views on the pragmatic management of newly-emerging trends of trade and modern technology on economic growth and society.
ASEAN-US Economic Conference (Kuala Lumpur)		November 18-20, 1981	The conference reviewed economic and political development and examined opportunities for cooperation in different fields of financing.
The United States, Japan, and Southeast Asia: the issues of interdependence (project)	East Asian Institute and International Economic Research Center of Columbia University	Multi-year project starting in 1982	The three broad aims of the project are: (1) to analyse export-oriented development strategies; (2) to analyse political and security relationships in the region and (3) to analyse the impact on bilateral US-Japan relationships of the policies pursued by Southeast Asian states.
ASEAN-US Dialogue (Washington D.C.)		March 9-11, 1982	The fourth meeting of the ASEAN-US Dialogue took place in the Department of State with the participation of several senior officials from ASEAN and the US.
Economic Basis of Pacific Security (Washington D.C.)	National Defence University	May 20-21, 1982	The conference was addressed by the Chairman of the House Foreign Affairs Committee and other government as well as academic representatives.

Conference on "ASEAN and Pacific Cooperation" (Bangkok, Thailand)	Pacific Cooperation Committee of Thailand under the direction of Deputy Prime Minister, Thanat Khoman	June 3-5, 1982	Coincided with a major ESCAP project on the same subject. Participants from ASEAN, the USA, New Zealand, Australia, Canada and Japan represented the academic, business and administrative sectors. This was the first semi-official conference organised by an ASEAN country.
Workshop on "Food and Development in the Pacific Basin" (Mexico City, Mexico)	Aspen Institute, Herbert H. Humphrey Institute, and Sistema Alimentario Mexicano (which is part of the office of the Presidency of Mexico)	June 10-12, 1982	Policy recommendations about domestic and international adjustments to food and agriculture to promote cooperation among nations of the region.
Food security in ASEAN: International Trade and Domestic Food Policies (Washington D.C.)	- East-West Center Resource Systems Institute - The Economic Research Service of the USDA	June 21, 1982	Pacific regional as well as national perspectives were presented by the team.
"Business Trends in the Pacific: A Conference on the Economic Outlook and Business Climate in Selected Asian Economies"	- PPCA - Wharton Econometric Forecasting Association	October 7, 1982	Emphasised the impact of policy developments and external events on Asian economies.
The Pacific Region in the year 2000	United Nations	November 17-18, 1982	One of the subjects discussed at the San Francisco Media roundtable on world issues.
The Pacific Community and American Interests	The Joint Center of Modern East Asia, University of Toronto / York University	November 23, 1982	A presentation was made by Ambassador Richard Sneider at this meeting, part of the on-going series sponsored by the Center.

Agri-Energy Roundtable Business Mission		Nov. 27-Dec. 11, 1982	Business development mission with on-site workshops in Saudi Arabia, Southeast Asia and Hawaii. The Singapore meeting dealt with "New Partners in Food/Energy Development; Southeast Asia, the Middle East and the West". The Hawaii meeting was on "Tropical Agriculture Roundup: New Partnership for Pacific Food Security".
PPCA Trade Roundtables	PPCA	1982	Series of meetings gathering senior US officials, businessmen and academics. Ambassador William E. Brock addressed the meeting held on Capitol Hill, December 2, 1982; subject of speech: "The GATT and its implications for Pacific Trade and Development".
Task Force on Pacific Cooperation	- Australian National University - Japan Special Committee for Pacific Cooperation - Korea Development Institute - Pacific Economic Cooperation Committee of Thailand	1982 - 1983	Four task forces were established by the Bangkok conference and will review problems related to trade and investments for the next conference to be held Bali at the end of year 1983.
Arizona Conference on Pacific Business and Law (Scottsdale, Arizona, USA)	- State Bar of Arizona - Arizona State University of Law - Pacific Basin Institute for Economic Development	February 4-5, 1983	Current legal dimensions of business relations with the PRC, the ASEAN nations, Hong Kong, Australia, and New Zealand.

Third International Symposium of JETRO	Japan External Trade Organisation	December 1-2, 1982	International conference with sessions that included: Industrialisation and the progress of Horizontal Economic Integration in the Developing Countries of the Asia-Pacific Area; and Industrial Complementation in Developing Countries (auto industry).
US National Committee Pacific Basin Economic Council	PBEC	January 13-14, 1983	Government officials met with US PBEC members to discuss and stress the importance of the Pacific region as a mainstay of the world economy and an open trading system.
13th PAFTAD Conference (Manila, Philippines)	PAFTAD, Asian Development Bank, Philippine Institute of Development Studies	January 24-28, 1983	Conference on the theme of "Energy and Structural Change in the Asia-Pacific Region".
Canada-Pacific Cooperation Committee (Ottawa)	PEC	February 5, 1983	Small group of businessmen - government and academics - met to prepare papers on Canadian interests and perspectives in the Pacific.
Conference on "Economic Cooperation Along the Pacific Rim"	University of Indiana, USA	March 24-25, 1983	Seminars on different social, political and economic aspects of Pacific Basin Cooperation.
International Standing Committee Pacific Basin Cooperation (PEC) (Bangkok)	PEC	May 23-24, 1983	Review first drafts of PEC Task Force papers.

Pacific Economic Cooperation Seminar	Centre for Strategic and International Studies, Georgetown University, Washington D.C.	Oct. 1983	Gathering of US Government representatives and international experts to discuss recent trends in Pacific economic cooperation.
Pacific Economic Cooperation Conference (Bali, Indonesia)	PEC	November 21-23, 1983	Meeting of Task Forces on Pacific Basin Cooperation to review analytic work and research in the area of more structured cooperation.

Conference on Pan-Pacific Cooperation
Bangkok, 3rd-5th June 1982

(The following is an unofficial summary of the Conference
by a European participant)

1.   Between 3rd and 5th June 1982, the ESCAP and the Pacific
Cooperation Committee of Thailand in Bangkok hosted a meeting of
Pacific Economic Cooperation. This meeting, which was
unofficially hosted by the Thai Government, under the sponsorship
of Thanat Khoman, Deputy Prime Minister, was a follow-up of the
1981 Canberra Conference on the same subject. Over 70
participants from 13 Pacific region countries attended this
conference.

2.   The conference itself was preceded by a meeting of experts
whose task it was to prepare the debates, propose recommendations
to the conference participants on the basis of the reports
prepared by the ESCAP. The experts were principally drawn from
among academics.

3.   On the first day of the meeting, four working groups were
formed by the experts:

    a) Trade and services
    b) Natural Resources
    c) Investment
    d) Institutional Aspects

4.   During the discussions, the following points were raised
concerning Pacific Basin cooperation:

    i)   the desire of the nations of the region to form
          macro-economic links (at government levels) and
          micro-economic links (at the level of the private
          sector) rather than creating a customs union or a block
          against the EEC;

    ii)   a regional concertation of trade that would not
          interfere with the GATT;

    iii) the necessity of planned structural adjustment in the
          industrial countries, and the NICs in order to create
          room for the 'third industrial wave' represented by the
          ASEAN;

    iv)   discussion of means to interest the sceptical ASEAN
          nations in larger regional planning exercises;

    v)   the possibility of the creation of an ASEBEX, similar in
          style to the STABEX.

Experts' Recommendations

5.   In the domain of <u>natural resources</u>, the experts outlined three principal areas: <u>energy security</u>; food security; forest and marine resources. In the first area, energy, they recommended that a better diffusion of energy conservation techniques be carried out, as well as substitutes for fossil energy sources. Linked to this was the problem of stock capacities.

6.   The ASEAN Food Security Reserve Agreement was proposed as a means of creating a regional plan for food. Experts felt that protectionist policies in agriculture were harmful to resource allocation, and more liberalised food and agricultural exchanges were proposed.

7.   Fish exploitation was discussed, and regional cooperation proposed for the management of availability.

8.   Underlining the economic take-off of the region after liberalisation of trade, the experts proposed more concrete measures to the conference for better regional cooperation:

- a ceiling on taxes levied by developing countries for manufactured goods (75% for example), in exchange for a more flexible import scheme on the part of developed countries for textile products;

- a better regional organisation of services linked to trade activities (insurance, freight, etc.).

9.   The experts recommended an end to the investment code war among developing countries (especially the tax on benefits clauses), and the hostile attitude towards transnational corporations; they also recommended more stable monetary agreements, liberalisation of markets and trade. These in fact reflect the positions of the developing countries throughout the world, and more specifically the positions of the Group of 77 in their recent proposals for global negotiations in the new round.

10.   The proposed institutional form of regional cooperation was the OPTAD arrangement. This would be reached in two stages:

1. regular conference meetings such as Canberra and Bangkok, to gather academics, businessmen and civil servants;

2. the creation of several 'task forces' which would study concrete proposals for cooperation. These groups would be financed by the host institution in which they were located.

Should the first two phases work, the steering committee of the operation could evolve into an OPTAD arrangement.

Conference

11.   The conference itself was divided into four sessions:

    1. presided by Thanat Khoman, presenting the experts'
       findings;
    2) presided by John Crawford) on interdependencies;
    3) presided by Ali Mutopo   )
    4) presided by Saburo Okita, on Pacific Basin Cooperation.

12.   Each of the 12 countries at the conference were represented
by an academic, a civil servant and a private sector participant.
Hong Kong, Taiwan and the People's Republic of China were absent.
(Two Taiwanese observers were present in a private capacity).

13.   The ASEAN was called upon by Crawford to make explicit
their fears for a more formal organisation in the region. The
political nature of the question rendered further discussion
difficult.

14.   The next conference site was fixed for Indonesia (Jakarta
1983). The proposal for a customs union was made by the
Philippines. Although more macro-economic cooperation was the aim
of the majority of interventions, no concrete proposal was made
for harmonisation of policy at the inter-governmental level.

15.   The last session, chaired by Mr. Okita, stressed the need
for a forum in the Pacific for the exchange of information and
policy. Although the long term was seen as a timeframe for an
eventual organisation, the idea of creating three task forces to
propose concrete measures of cooperation to the next meeting in
Jakarta was endorsed. It was also suggested that the steering
committee could represent the interests of the region in global
negotiations, at least as an observer (GATT).

16.   Three task forces were formed:

    1. Manufactured goods (to be organised by the Korea
       Development Institute)

    2. Raw materials:

        i) agriculture (to be organised by the PEC of
           Thailand)
       ii) minerals (to be organised by the Australian
           National University

    3. Investment and technology transfer (to be organised by
       the Special Committee for Cooperation, Japan).

These groups are charged with maintaining and undertaking liaison
activities with other research institutions, and coordinating
research in the area of their speciality (tripartite, academics,
business).

17.   South Korea proposed Seoul as a site for the fourth
conference in 1985.

18.   It would appear that the reservations of the ASEAN group
are diminishing. This could be the most substantial progress to
date on Pacific cooperation.

19.   As a result of the conference, a group of six leading
personalities in the Pacific Basin were assigned to an
'inter-conference working group' to organise the Jakarta
conference. The six are: Thailand's Deputy Prime Minister,
Thanat Khoman; Indonesia's Minister of Information, Gen Ali
Murtopo; Japan's Advisor to the Foreign Ministry, Saburo Okita;
Australia's John Crawford, Chancellor of the National University;
US Former Ambassador, Richard Schneider, and South Korea's Former
Prime Minister, Nahm Duk Woo.

20.   It is significant that developing countries in the region
now appear to be taking a much more active role in promoting the
idea of Pacific Basin cooperation, and that in many respects the
future of the concept is in the hands of the 'third wave' nations
of the region.

LIST OF PARTICIPANTS, BANGKOK

Chairman: H.E. Dr. Thanat Khoman
Deputy Prime Minister of Thailand
Assisted by Dr. Narongchai Akrasanee, ESCAP

Australia Sir John Crawford
Chancellor
Australian National University

Mr. Alan Brown
Head
Economic Division
Department of Foreign Affairs

Sir James Vernon
Chairman
Pacific Basin Economic Council

Canada Mr. Eric Trigg
Executive Vice President
Alcan Aluminium Ltd.

Professor H.E. English
Carleton University

Mr. W.T. Delworth
Assistant Secretary for Asia and the Pacific
Ministry of External Affairs

Chile Mr. Oscar Fuentes
Minister Counsellor
Chilean Embassy to Japan

Professor Francisco Orrego
Academic Sector

Mr. Juan Rueter
Economical Sector

Indonesia Dr. Hadi Soesastro
CSIS

General Ali Murtopo
Minister of Information

Dr. Faud Hasan
Director
Research and Planning Department
Ministry of Foreign Affairs

Japan	Dr. Saburo Okita Chairman Institute for Domestic and International Policy Studies Adivsor, Ministry of Foreign Affairs
	Mr. Noburo Gotoh Chairman and President Tokyu Corporation Ltd.
	Professor Seizaburo Sato The University of Tokyo
Korea, Republic of	Dr. Kim Kih Wan Director Korea Development Institute
	Professor Han Sung-Joo Korea University
	Mr. Suh Kyung Suk Ambassador At Large Ministry of Foreign Affairs
Malaysia	Mr. Choo Eng Guan Principal Assistant Secretary Ministry of Foreign Affairs
	Professor Paul Chan University of Malaya
	Dr. Datuk Mohkzani Executive Director United Motor Works (Malaysia) Holdings Berhad
New Zealand	Professor Richard Manning Economics Department University of Canterbury
	Mr. D.K. McDowell Assistant Secretary for Asia and Pacific Ministry of Foreign Affairs
	Mr. John Fair Private Sector Participant
Philippines	Mr. Samuel T. Ramel Executive Officer ASEAN National Co-ordinating Agency
	Mr. David Sycip President Rizal Banking Corporation

Professor Carlos P. Ramos
University of the Philippines

Singapore   Mr. K. Kesavapany
Deputy Director
Ministry of Foreign Affairs

Professor Tham Seong Chee
National University of Singapore

Mr. Lim Ho Hup
President
ASEAN Finance Corporation

Thailand   Dr. Snoh Unakul
Secretary General
NESDB

Professor Somsak Xuto
National Institute for Development Administration

Mr. Chote Sophonpanich
Senior Executive Vice President
Bangkok Bank Ltd.

United States   Mr. Anthony C. Albrecht
Deputy Assistant Secretary of State for
    East Asia and Pacific Affairs
Department of State

Ambassador Richard Sneider
Chairman of Executive Committee
Pan Pacific Community Association
Washington, D.C.

Dr. Mark Earle
SRI International
California

ESCAP   H.E. S.A.M.S. Kibria
Executive Secretary

Mr. Koji Nakagawa
Deputy Executive Secretary

Mr. Edward Van Roy
Officer-in-Charge
Development Planning Division

Observers   Professor Heinz Arndt
Australian National University

Professor Peter Drysdale
Australian National University

Senator Hugh Scott
Chairman of Board of Directors
Pan Pacific Community Association

Mr. Alexander Pires
Pan Pacific Community Association

Dr. Mark Borthwick
Executive Director
Pan Pacific Community Association

Mr. Takashi Onda
Director of Financial Affairs Division
Ministry of Foreign Affairs
Tokyo

Admiral Lloyd R. Vasey
President
Pacific Forum
Honolulu, Hawaii

Mr. Kobo Inamura
Japanese Embassy
Bangkok

Mr. Akiyoshi Miura
Manager
Policy and Planning Officer
Tokyo Corporation

Mr. Chang-choon Lee
Presidential Secretary in Political and
    Foreign Affairs
Office of the President (The Blue House)
Seoul, Korea

Miss Chow Kit Boey
Development Planning Division, ESCAP

Mrs. Mingsarn Kaosa-ard
Statistic Division, ESCAP

Dr. Nimit Nontapantawat
Vice President
Bangkok Bank

Mr. Bunlue Chantadissi
Assistant Vice President
Bangkok Bank

Mr. Robert Oxnam
President
Asia Society
New York, N.Y.

Mr. Minoru Kubota
Counsellor
Japanese Embassy
Bangkok

Mr. John E. Buckley (or L.T. Cleary)
First Secretary
Australian Embassy
Bangkok

Ms. Siriporn Bhathakul
Ministry of Foreign Affairs
Bangkok

Professor Hans Indorf
Faculty of Political Science
Chulalongkorn University
Bangkok

Dr. Chulscheeb Chinwanno
Assistant Professor
Mahidul University

Miss Pranee Saipiroon
Researcher
Political Sciences Faculty
Chulalongkorn University

M.R. Sukhumbhan Boripatra
Lecturer
Political Sciences Faculty
Chulalongkorn University

Dr. Vinita Sukraset
Assistant Professor
Political Sciences Faculty
Chulalongkorn University

Mr. Masakiko Ebashi
Director
Japan Trade Center (JETRO)
Manila

OECD SALES AGENTS
DÉPOSITAIRES DES PUBLICATIONS DE L'OCDE

OECD PUBLICATIONS, 2, rue André-Pascal, 75775 PARIS CEDEX 16 - No. 42681 1983
PRINTED IN FRANCE
(41 83 03 1) ISBN 92-64-12483-7